THE QUEEN'S OWN ROYAL WEST KENT REGIMENT 1951 - 1961

Lieutenant-Colonel
H. D. CHAPLIN

THE REGIMENTAL MUSEUM COMMITTEE

Published by
THE QUEEN'S OWN MUSEUM COMMITTEE
The Barracks,
Maidstone
1964

THIS book, the final volume of the history of The Queen's Own Royal West Kent Regiment, is dedicated to the everlasting memory of the fourteen members of The Queen's Own who gave their lives on Active Service during the years 1946 to 1961.

Their names are inscribed in a small Book of Remembrance, which is in All Saints' Church, Maidstone.

FOREWORD

This volume of the history of The Queen's Own Royal West Kent Regiment covers the period from 1951 to 1961 when the regiment was amalgamated with The Buffs (Royal East Kent Regiment) to form The Queen's Own Buffs, The Royal Kent Regiment. Although, after the amalgamation, the Territorial and Cadet battalions of The Queen's Own were left to carry on the old title, Amalgamation Day on 1st March, 1961, virtually signified the end of an era.

Nevertheless, all of us in the old Queen's Own can and should look forward with confidence to the future. The Queen's Own Buffs, The Royal Kent Regiment is not a new regiment but a continuation of two very old regiments with long and distinguished records and it will thus perpetuate all that was best in both. As the County Regiment of Kent it will undoubtedly be a worthy heir, but it will need the staunch support of all those connected with both old regiments—not only those who are still serving but, in particular, the old comrades.

This will be the third volume of the history of The Queen's Own which has been written by Lieutenant-Colonel H. D. Chaplin, the Regimental Historian, and all of us who have served in the regiment owe him a tremendous debt of gratitude.

D. E. B. TALBOT, *Major-General,*

Colonel, The Queen's Own Royal West Kent Regiment.

ERRATA

On page 7, 25th line, List of Battle Honours, for "TERMINOLI" read "TERMOLI"

Preface

IT was as long ago as 1782 that The 3rd (The Buffs) and The 50th Regiments of Foot became associated with the county of Kent, the former with East Kent and the latter with West Kent. The relevant letter to the Colonel of The 50th, dated August 31, 1782, read:

> "His Majesty having been pleased to order that The 50th Regiment of Foot, which you command, should take the county name of The 50th or West Kent Regiment, and be looked upon as attached to that division of the county.
>
> I am to acquaint you that it is His Majesty's further pleasure that you should, in all things, conform to that idea and endeavour by all means in your power to improve that connection, so as to create a mutual attachment between the county and the regiment."

In 1873 Kent was divided into two military sub-districts. Eight years later these sub-districts became The 3rd and The 50th Regimental Districts, which were in fact respectively the recruiting areas of The Buffs (Royal East Kent Regiment) and The Queen's Own Royal West Kent Regiment. But the boundary between them was not the River Medway, which divides East from West Kent; it was an arbitrary line some distance east of it. In this way the recruiting areas of the two regiments of Kent were clearly defined, the Depot of The Buffs being established at Canterbury and that of The Queen's Own at Maidstone.

When, in 1957, the Army Council decided that fifteen pairs of infantry regiments must be amalgamated, one pair was The Buffs (Royal East Kent Regiment) and The Queen's Own Royal West

Kent Regiment. The amalgamation took place on March 1, 1961. Thus, after being associated each with a "division of the county" for nearly 180 years, the two regiments were merged to form a single regiment of Kent.

The purpose of the present volume is to describe the last ten years of The Queen's Own before the amalgamation. The general history of the regiment during that period (1951-1961) is recorded in chapters 1 and 3. The story of the 1st Battalion on active service in Malaya, Egypt and Cyprus is told in chapters 2 and 4. Chapter 5 deals with the amalgamation. In appendices B (Part 1), F, G, H and J attempts have been made to elucidate some aspects of the history of the regiment not fully covered in previous volumes.

Readers will find that the Home Counties Group of Regiments is mentioned several times in the text. As some of them may not be familiar with that term, an explanation of the so-called "Group System" may be desirable. During the 1939-1945 War it was found to be impossible always to post a man to a battalion of the regiment for which he had enlisted. So, in 1946, the Army Council resolved that infantry regiments would be grouped geographically and that every infantryman should accept the liability to serve in any regiment in his group besides his own. The Queen's Own was placed in the Home Counties Group, later known as the Home Counties Brigade. So it came about that during the period under review there was serving with the 1st Battalion The Queen's Own a considerable number of individuals who belonged to the regiments of Surrey, East Kent, London,[1] Sussex and Middlesex.

As a rule, initials have been omitted from the text except when they are necessary to distinguish individuals with the same name. They can be found, if wanted, in the Personal Index at the end of the book. A General Index has not been included because events can be readily traced by reference to the chapter summaries in the table of Contents.

Some errors in other works concerning the history of the regiment have come to light. The necessary amendments are in Appendix K.

H. D. CHAPLIN.

[1] The Royal Fusiliers (City of London Regiment).

Acknowledgments

THE historical background to the emergencies in Malaya, Egypt and Cyprus has been obtained from the following works, to the authors and publishers of which I am indebted:—

Malaya, the Facts Behind the Fighting. Colonial Office, 1952.

Handbook to Malaya and the Emergency. Department of Information, Federation of Malaya, 1953.

The Most Important Country by John Connell. Cassell and Company Ltd., 1957.

Operations in Egypt, November to December 1956. Despatch by General Sir Charles F. Keightley. (Supplement to *The London Gazette,* 10th September 1957.)

Cyprus, the Dispute and the Settlement. Royal Institute of International Affairs, 1959.

Cyprus. Central Office of Information, 1960.

Cyprus Guerrilla by Doros Alastos. Heinemann, 1960.

The Memoirs of Sir Anthony Eden: Full Circle. Cassell and Company Ltd., 1960.

In telling the story of the 1st Battalion in Malaya, Egypt and Cyprus I was greatly assisted by accounts written by the various commanding officers. Many articles and descriptions of events in the regimental journal, *The Queen's Own Gazette,* also gave me much help.

My thanks are due to the last editor of *The Queen's Own Gazette* for permission to reproduce the illustrations, which originally appeared in that journal.

Finally, I wish to express my gratitude to Major-General R. A. Riddell, C.B.E., and Lieutenant-Colonel H. N. Edwards, M.B.E., D.L., for reading over and criticising the first draft of this book.

Contents

MAPS

ILLUSTRATIONS

CHAPTER 1

Resurgence

January 1951 — June 1956

1. *Regimental*

In January 1951 the state of The Queen's Own Royal West Kent Regiment was as follows:

Colonel-in-Chief	H.R.H. The Duchess of Kent.
Colonel	Major-General W. P. Oliver.
Regimental Depot	Maidstone.
1st Battalion (50th and 97th)	Shorncliffe (for Malaya).
3rd Battalion (Militia)	In suspended animation.
4th/5th Battalion (T.A.)	Headquarters at Tonbridge.

A roll of Colonels, Commanding Officers and Depot Commanders from 1951 to 1961 is given in Appendix A.

The Regimental Depot was not active, since no recruits were being trained there. The 1st Battalion was re-organising as a normal Line battalion, having relinquished the non-operational role of Basic Training Unit for the Home Counties Group of Regiments a few weeks back. Both the Depot and the 1st Battalion were soon to resume their traditional roles, giving a sense of resurgence to the regiment.

The stream of regimental events was rippled by the war in Korea, which had started in June 1950. The immediate effect was that some of The Queen's Own were attached to the 1st Battalion The Middlesex Regiment in Korea. These included Major Dowse, Lieutenants Osborne and Bosworth, C.S.Ms Copper and Seabrook, Sergeant Bailey, ten Regular rank and file, and 31 National Servicemen. Later, a number of Queen's Own Reservists were recalled to the Colours and served in Korea with the 1st Battalion The Royal Fusiliers and the 1st Battalion The Gloucestershire Regiment. Major Thomas went on to the Staff of the 1st Commonwealth Division. Private Page was killed while serving with The Middlesex Regiment.[1] Sergeant Levy and Lance-Corporal Healey were wounded when with The Royal Fusiliers. For a list of Honours and Awards see Appendix B.

A long-term effect of the war in Korea was that the period of National Service was increased from 18 months to two years.

The Book of Remembrance for the 1,678 members of the regiment, who gave their lives in the Second World War, was placed in All Saints' Church, Maidstone, on July 15, 1951. It was handed to the vicar, Canon C. B. Sampson, for safe-keeping by the Colonel of the Regiment at the customary Memorial Service held during the Annual Reunion of The Past and Present Association.

The Regimental Museum, which had recently been re-opened in the former Mobilisation Store at the Depot, was visited by the Mayor and Mayoress of Maidstone (Alderman and Mrs. B. J. Watson) and members of the Corporation on September 24. They were shown round by the Curator, Major Love, and were entertained by officers of the regiment.

With the re-activisation of the Depot in June 1951, the Regimental Cricket Week took a more important place in the life of The Queen's Own. Matches were usually played against such teams as The Buffs, The Queen's Royal Regiment, The Mote, The Band of Brothers and The Babes.

On the death of His Majesty King George VI at Sandringham on February 6, 1952, the Colonel of the Regiment sent a telegram to the Private Secretary of Her Majesty Queen Elizabeth conveying the deepest sympathy of all ranks of The Queen's Own and of The Past and Present Association. The following reply was received: "Would you please convey to all ranks, Past and Present, of the

[1]The Roll of Honour is on pages 109 and 110

Regimental Association Her Majesty's deep appreciation of their message of sympathy."

For the funeral of King George VI, which took place on February 15, there were no detachments of the regiment in London. The only member of The Queen's Own to take an official part was Brigadier Riddell who, as A.D.C. to the King, marched in the procession. At Maidstone a Memorial Service in All Saints' Church was attended by troops from the Depot. The 4th/5th Battalion provided buglers and drummers to sound "The Last Post" and "Reveille" at a Memorial Service in Tonbridge Parish Church.

The Home Guard was re-formed in April 1952. Of the 33 battalions raised in Kent, 16 were affiliated to The Queen's Own and wore the cap badge. A list of these, with the names of the commanding officers, can be found in Appendix D. The enthusiasm with which the Home Guardsmen attended courses at the Depot and Rifle Meetings in inclement weather, filled their instructors with astonishment. It was typical of their spirit that the battalions sent contributions to *The Queen's Own Gazette*. Brigadier Ingham, as a re-employed officer, was G.S.O. 1 (Home Guard) at Eastern Command. The Home Guard was placed on a reserve basis in the spring of 1956.

Early in 1952 Colonel Chitty, late of The Queen's Own, was appointed County Commandant of the Army Cadet Force. Lieutenant-Colonel Durtnell, also a retired officer of the regiment, became Assistant Commandant; he supervised the four Cadet battalions which were affiliated to The Queen's Own. These were: the 1st at Sidcup, the 2nd at Swanley, the 3rd at Tunbridge Wells and the 4th at Maidstone.[1] They usually assembled once a year at the Regimental Depot to compete in their annual competitions. Their boxing tournaments were sometimes held in the Depot gymnasium.

The posthumous Victoria Cross won by Lance-Corporal Harman at Kohima in April 1944 was presented by his father, Mr. M. C. Harman, to the regiment at a parade at the Depot on August 15, 1952. This decoration was placed in a position of honour in the Regimental Museum.

Another Victoria Cross was acquired in 1953, when that won by Sergeant Coleman at Sevastopol was bought by members of the 1st

[1]These four Cadet battalions were in 1959 re-organised into one unit with headquarters at Tonbridge. Major Elmslie, formerly of the 4th Battalion (T.A.), was the commanding officer.

Battalion as a memorial to those of the battalion who died on active service in Malaya. This decoration was officially handed by Brevet-Lieutenant-Colonel Crook into the safe-keeping of the Regimental Museum at the 16th Annual Reunion in June 1954. It had been hoped that Mrs. Pauline Coleman, a relative of Sergeant Coleman, would be present at the ceremony. But she was unable to travel from the North of England. She gave to the Museum the War Office letter, dated November 17, 1858, which covered the despatch to Sergeant Coleman's family of his V.C. and medals after his death in Delhi.

The custom of placing a wreath at the foot of Nelson's Column in Trafalgar Square on October 21 each year was resumed in 1952. The custom began in 1922 to commemorate the period in 1794 when The 50th Foot served with Nelson in Corsica. It had lapsed during the Second World War. (See Appendix H. "Nelson and The Queen's Own.")

The Colonel-in-Chief and her elder son, The Duke of Kent, made a tour of the Far East in the autumn of 1952. The Colonel of the Regiment was among those to bid Her Royal Highness farewell at London Airport. Major Buckle[1] acted as her A.D.C. during the tour. At Singapore on October 4 the Duchess received the officers of the regiment, who were on the Staff there, and their wives at a private cocktail party given for them by His Excellency The Governor. The Duchess and her son then went to Malaya to visit the 1st Battalion at Kuala Kubu Bharu (See Chapter 2, Section 7). At Hong Kong on October 30 the four officers and 30 other ranks of the regiment, who were stationed there, were presented to Her Royal Highness at the N.A.A.F.I. Club at Kowloon. Several of the other ranks had served with The Middlesex Regiment in Korea; she had a special word to say to them. During her visit to the colony "A Hundred Pipers" was frequently heard on Radio Hong Kong.

On her return from the tour of the Far East, Her Royal Highness attended a banquet given in her honour by the British Government at the Mansion House on December 16. The Guard of Honour was provided by the Regimental Depot. It consisted of recruits in their fourth week of training and some of the Permanent Staff—a total of 70 other ranks. The Guard Commander was Captain Fletcher; Lieutenant Howlett carried the Queen's Colour.[2] After a final rehearsal

[1]Son of Major M. P. Buckle, D.S.O., of The Queen's Own, who was killed at Neuve Chapelle in October 1914.

[2]The Queen's Colour of the 2nd Battalion which was at the Depot for safe-keeping.

THE COLONEL-IN-CHIEF INSPECTING THE GUARD OF HONOUR AT THE MANSION HOUSE, 16TH DECEMBER, 1952.

THE DEPOT CORONATION CONTINGENT, JUNE, 1953.

GENERAL VIEW OF THE REGIMENTAL MUSEUM AT THE DEPOT, MAY, 1952.

with the band of The Royal Fusiliers, the guard had entrained at Maidstone West Station for London on the evening of the 15th. The night had been spent at the Tower of London. For the occasion, permission had been given by the Lord Mayor for the guard to march through the City with fixed bayonets. Her Royal Highness was met by the Colonel of the Regiment, who presented Captain Fletcher. The guard returned to Maidstone in the evening.

To commemorate the visit of Her Royal Highness to her regiment on active service in Malaya, a painting of her was purchased by the officers. It was hung in the ante-room of the officers' mess at the Regimental Depot. A larger portrait of the Duchess, specially painted by Simon Elwes, was presented by Major Druce, a retired officer, to the regiment and was placed in the dining room of the Depot officers' mess. This portrait was hung at the Royal Academy's Summer Exhibition at Burlington House, London, in 1954. A reproduction of it was used as a frontispiece for *The Queen's Own Royal West Kent Regiment, 1920-1950.*[1]

The Colonel of the Regiment embarked on February 21, 1953, to take up the appointment of Principal Staff Officer to General Sir Gerald Templer, High Commissioner in Malaya. A year later he became General Officer Commanding Berlin (British Sector). During his absence overseas, Brigadier Riddell acted as Deputy Colonel.

For the Coronation of Queen Elizabeth II on June 2, 1953, the regiment had four contingents in London. Two of them were accommodated at Olympia and marched in the procession. The other two were accommodated in a tented camp in Kensington Gardens and lined portions of the route. The marching contingents were: Captain Sivers (in command), Captain Dodson (carrying the Queen's Colour), Lieutenant Lygo (carrying the Regimental Colour) and seven other ranks of the 1st Battalion, who had come from Malaya for the occasion; and Major A. R. H. Waring and four other ranks of the 4th/5th. Lieutenant Howlett and nine other ranks from the Depot lined a portion of the route in Park Lane near Apsley House. Lieutenant Duggan (carrying the Queen's Colour) and 17 other ranks of the 4th/5th were in position in East Carriage Drive near

[1]These two portraits were transferred in 1961 to the officers' mess of the 1st Battalion The Queen's Own Buffs, The Royal Kent Regiment. Major Druce was commissioned into The Queen's Own in October 1894 and retired in 1913.

Hyde Park Corner. Brigadier Riddell marched in the procession and was in Westminster Abbey. Six seats or standing places were allotted to members of The Past and Present Association in Hyde Park. At Tonbridge the drums of the 4th/5th, wearing scarlet uniform, beat Retreat in the grounds of the Castle. At Maidstone, where Week Street was decorated with wooden models of soldiers of The Queen's Own in period costumes, a Coronation Dance was held in the Depot gymnasium.

On the Sunday after the Coronation, troops from the Depot took part in a Coronation Parade at Maidstone and attended a special service in All Saints' Church.

A Coronation Ex-Servicemen's Review was held in Hyde Park on Sunday July 5. The Queen's Own contingent, which was commanded by Colonel Clay, was 84 strong, including seven standard bearers. After a short service, Her Majesty The Queen drove down the ranks in a specially-appointed Land Rover. Her Majesty then addressed the parade. Three cheers were given. The ceremony ended with a march past.

Colonel Palmer, Chairman of The Past and Present Association, died in June 1953. He was succeeded by Lieutenant-Colonel Edwards. A plaque to the memory of Colonel Palmer was placed in All Saints' Church. A memorial tablet to Colonel Buchanan-Dunlop, the previous Chairman, had been placed in the church in July 1952. (See Appendix J for an account of The Past and Present Association.)

The Haifa lectern[1] was moved from the Garrison Church, Shorncliffe, to the Regimental Depot in November 1953. Thereafter, it was used at services held for recruits and their relatives after Passing-Out Parades and during At Homes.

The Militia, which had been in suspended animation since July 1919, was disbanded by Army Order 47 of 1953. The final disbandment of the 3rd Battalion (Militia) The Queen's Own took place in the autumn of 1954. Much of its silver was in use at the Regimental Depot. Its Colours remained in the Regimental Museum.

The El Alamein Memorial was unveiled by Field-Marshal Viscount

[1]This lectern had been placed in the Garrison Chapel at Peninsula Barracks, Haifa, in memory of those members of the 2nd Battalion who lost their lives in Palestine in 1938. It had been brought to England in 1948. See page 107 of "The Queen's Own Royal West Kent Regiment, 1920-1950."

Montgomery on October 24, 1954. It commemorates the officers and other ranks of the armies and air forces of the Commonwealth who fell in Egypt and Libya from December 1940 to July 1942; in the Battles of Alam el Halfa and El Alamein; in the advance to the frontier of Tunisia; and in the campaigns of 1941 in Iraq, Syria, the Lebanon and Persia. On it are inscribed the names of those officers and other ranks who have no known graves; 45 of these were members of The Queen's Own. In a cemetery nearby are buried over 7,000 officers and men in named graves; 90 of these graves are of members of the regiment.

At the end of 1954 a Committee was set up at the War Office to draw up recommendations to govern the award of Battle Honours for the 1939-1945 War. Its report was submitted to the Army Council six months later, and a Regimental Committee was formed under the chairmanship of Brigadier Talbot to select the Battle Honours to be claimed by The Queen's Own. Forty-eight Honours were eventually decided on, ten of which were to be inscribed on the Queen's Colour. They were approved by the Army Council in the spring of 1957. The list was:

> "Defence of the Escaut,"[1] "Foret de Nieppe," "NORTH-WEST EUROPE, 1940," "Alam el Halfa," "EL ALAMEIN," "Djebel Abiod," "Djebel Azzag, 1942," "Oued Zarga," "Djebel Ang," "MEDJEZ PLAIN," "Longstop Hill, 1943," "Si Abdallah," "North Africa, 1942-43," "CENTURIPE," "Monte Rivoglia," Sicily, 1943," "Terminoli," "San Salvo," "THE SANGRO," "Romagnoli," Impossible Bridge," "Villa Grande," "CASSINO," "Castle Hill," "Liri Valley," "Piedimonte Hill," "TRASIMENE LINE," "Arrezzo," "Advance to Florence," Monte Scalari," "Casa Fortis,"[2] "Rimini Line," "Savio Bridgehead," "Monte Pianoereno," "Monte Spaduro," "The Senio," "ARGENTA GAP," "Italy, 1943-45," "Greece, 1944-45," "Leros," "MALTA, 1940-42," "North Arakan," "Razabil," "Mayu Tunnels," "DEFENCE OF KOHIMA," "Taungtha," "Sittang, 1945," "Burma, 1943-45."

The Battle Honours for the Queen's Colour are in capitals.

The Colonel of the Regiment became Vice-Chief of the Imperial

[1] "The Escaut" is another name for the River Scheldt.

[2] "Casa Fortis" is the name of the action fought by the 1st Battalion at the Canal di Rivaldino during the capture of Forli.

General Staff in May 1955, with the rank of Lieutenant-General. He was made a K.C.B. in the Queen's Birthday Honours List in 1956.

To mark the centenary of the fall of Sevastopol, a memorial service was held in All Saints' Church, Maidstone, on Sunday, September 11, 1955. The sermon was preached by The Very Reverend Hedley Burrows, Dean of Hereford, a relative of Captain Hedley Vicars, of The 97th, who lost his life during the campaign. The Depot troops attended the service at full strength. Members of The Past and Present Association, including standard bearers, were there. On the previous night a dance was held at the Depot. The Dean of Hereford, who stayed at the Depot for the week-end, was present and spoke to a number of men.

General Sir Charles Bonham-Carter, G.C.B., C.M.G., D.S.O., who had been Colonel of the Regiment from September 1936 until September 1946, died at his home, Durford Height, Petersfield, on October 21, 1955.

The re-organisation of Anti-Aircraft Command in 1955 caused a drastic reduction in the Royal Artillery of the Territorial Army. In the Blackheath area, four regiments were reduced to one battery each. One of these regiments was 569 (The Queen's Own) (M) L.A.A./S.L. Regiment (T.A.), which was affiliated to The Queen's Own. It became Q (The Queen's Own) Battery of 265 Light Anti-Aircraft Regiment (T.A.). This battery remained affiliated to the regiment, its headquarters still being at Holly Hedge House, Blackheath.

A close liaison was maintained with the allied regiments of the Dominions. In 1950 (just before the period under review) The Queen's Own gave a silver rose bowl to The Canterbury Regiment of New Zealand to mark the re-constitution of that regiment after the 1939-45 War. The official presentation was made at the first post-war officers' dinner at Christchurch by Colonel Talbot, who was then on the United Kingdom Liaison Staff in New Zealand. In the spring of 1952 Colonel Pulverman and Major Turner visited the company of The Carleton and York Regiment, which was serving with the 27th Canadian Infantry Brigade in Germany. The company commander presented a red beret with their regimental badge to the Museum. In July 1952 Major Read, who was at the Canadian School of Infantry in Ontario at the time, attended a combined operations exercise carried out by The Kent Regiment.

In return, members of the allied regiments, whenever they were in England, made a point of liaising with The Queen's Own. In May 1953 Major-General Sir Howard Kippenberger and Lieutenant Corrigan of The Canterbury Regiment were guests at the Regimental Dinner at the United Service Club in London. General Kippenberger also attended the 15th Annual Reunion in July and placed a wreath at the foot of the Regimental Cenotaph in Brenchley Gardens on behalf of The Canterbury Regiment. From the same regiment, Major Baker attended the 16th Reunion in 1954, and Lieut. Quigley visited the Depot in 1955. Sergeant Moore of The Carleton and York Regiment was at the Coronation Dance at the Depot in June 1953. Of The Kent Regiment, Sergeant Simpson visited the Depot in 1954 and Majors Beardall and Merritt in 1955.

The Canadian Militia was re-organised in 1954, when several regiments were amalgamated. The Carleton and York Regiment was merged with The New Brunswick Regiment to form the 1st New Brunswick Regiment (Carleton and York). The Kent Regiment became The Essex and Kent Scottish. In June 1956 the 1st New Brunswick Regiment was made a Royal regiment, Her Majesty Queen Elizabeth II being its Colonel-in-Chief.

2. *The Regimental Depot*

When Regimental Depots were re-activated in 1951, the Group Training Centres were closed. They were replaced by Brigade Depots, where National Servicemen, having completed their basic training at Regimental Depots, trained for four weeks if they were destined for the Middle East, or for ten weeks if they were to be posted to a battalion in Malaya or Korea. In addition, these Brigade Depots trained potential leaders. Each was commanded by a Brigade Colonel, who also supervised the training policy of the Regimental Depots in his brigade, as a group was now called. In the Home Counties, the Brigade Depot was established at Canterbury.

The first intake of National Servicemen to be trained under the new system assembled at the Regimental Depot at Maidstone on June 21, 1951. There were 103 of them. This was more than had been expected. But for two months beforehand large quantities of clothing, stores and equipment had been arriving, and the Quartermaster, Major Pond, was equal to the occasion. The Orderly Room Staff, the Medical Officer, the Tailor and the Barber had a busy day.

After six weeks' basic training, the first intake passed out at a parade taken by the Colonel of the Regiment. The parade was watched by some 80 relatives and friends of the recruits. Afterwards, there was a short service in the gymnasium, followed by tea in the drill shed. The draft left for Canterbury by train on August 2. It returned from the 1st Battalion in Malaya for release in June 1953.

The system was altered in November 1952. From then onwards National Servicemen were trained for ten weeks at the Regimental Depot and were sent direct from there to the 1st Battalion in Malaya. In March 1953 there were four squads under training at the Depot, a total of 133 recruits. All except 13 of them lived in Kent. The fathers of ten of them had served in The Queen's Own.

The demolition of the last wooden barrack blocks at the Depot was completed in February 1951. The soil on which they had stood was raked over; many coins and several relics were found, some dating back to the days when the barracks were occupied by the 7th Light Dragoons. After this, the only original wooden building remaining at the Depot was the officers' mess block.

For the Proclamation of Her Majesty Queen Elizabeth II on February 7, 1952, the Depot marched at full strength with fixed bayonets to the Town Hall, where the troops formed up in three sides of a square in front of a dais. After the Proclamation had been read by the Mayor of Maidstone, three cheers were given for the Queen.

Inter-squad boxing competitions for the Durtnell Shield were re-started in February 1952. Another trophy competed for by the squads was the Simpson Cup, which was now presented for a combination of all games and sports, including the log obstacle course and struggle-ball. Medals were given to the recruits with the highest scores at shooting. The Permanent Staff competed at shooting for the Neve Cup, which was presented in memory of Major Neve by his wife[1] The first winner was R.S.M. Hayley in 1953.

The Depot was honoured by a visit from the Colonel-in-Chief on Sunday May 4, 1952. In the Regimental Museum Lance-Corporals Pannell and Martin, who had recently been decorated for gallantry

[1]Major Neve died of wounds in Hong Kong in January 1942.

THE PROCLAMATION OF QUEEN ELIZABETH II AT MAIDSTONE, 7TH FEBRUARY, 1952.

THE MAYOR OF MAIDSTONE LAYING A WREATH AT THE REGIMENTAL CENOTAPH DURING THE 17TH ANNUAL REUNION, 24TH JULY, 1955.

in Malaya, were presented to Her Royal Highness. Members of the Permanent Staff and their wives were presented to her in the sergeants' mess. She was entertained at luncheon in the officers' mess by the Colonel of the Regiment and officers of the Depot.

An unusual intake arrived in July 1952. It consisted of the editors of nearly all the Kent newspapers. They came to find out what life was really like for National Servicemen during their first few weeks in the army. They were met by the Colonel of the Regiment, who took them to see recruits receiving instruction in various subjects. They were particularly interested in the work of the Personnel Selection Officer, whose duty it was to suggest suitable military employment for each man according to his abilities. Major Love took them round the Regimental Museum, which greatly pleased them. They lunched in the officers' mess. The reports in their papers about the day's visit showed that their impression had been favourable.

The cafeteria system with trays for meals was introduced in the dining hall in January 1953. Another innovation was the painting in each barrack room of a shield depicting the Maidstone crest with a photograph of the Freedom Cup and Citation, which had been given to the regiment in August 1944. Television was installed in the N.A.A.F.I. in February 1955.

The annual Hardy Cup Boxing Competition between The Queen's Own recruits and those of The Buffs was revived in January 1953, when the bouts were fought at Maidstone. The Buffs brought a host of spectators, and all messes were At Home to them. The Queen's Own won by five fights to two. Subsequently, victory usually went to The Buffs.

A Depot Rifle Meeting was held in June 1953 at Hythe, whither the troops went in buses. This became almost an annual event. Classification and other shooting were usually done on Milton Ranges at Gravesend, or sometimes at Lower Halstow.

When the 1st Battalion marched through Maidstone on April 1, 1954, after its return from Malaya, recruits of the Depot lined the route. Members of the Permanent Staff were on duty at the enclosures for spectators. Further information about this march can be found in the next section.

The Permanent Staff received instruction in the Belgian 7.62 mm.

F.N. Automatic Rifle in October 1955 from an instructor from the Small Arms School.

Two results of competitions were notable. The Depot cross-country team of seven runners was fourth in the Home Counties District race in February 1954. The shooting team won the Inter-Depot Open Match at the Home Counties Rifle Meeting in May 1956.

3. *The 1st Battalion at Singapore, Maidstone and Luneburg*

The 1st Battalion, less the advanced party, sailed in the troopship "Devonshire" from Liverpool at 6.20 p.m. on February 2, 1951. In the Bay of Biscay both engines were put out of action in a gale. An SOS was sent out, but the ship's crew repaired the damage in three hours. Except for a few minor injuries, the troops stood the ordeal very well. In the Mediterranean, the sea was calm and the weather pleasantly warm. There was no shore leave at Port Said because there was a suspected case of chickenpox on board. A few hours were spent on shore at Colombo, where the men, in neatly-pressed jungle green drill uniform, were able to post food parcels home. Food rationing was still in force in the United Kingdom.

The battalion disembarked at Singapore on March 3, and went by lorry to a tented camp at Nee Soon in the centre of the island. The first few days were spent in drawing jungle equipment and handing in battle dress. Vehicles, wireless sets, etc. had already been obtained by the Quartermaster, Captain Sivers, who had arrived with the advanced party. Also with this party, which was commanded by Major Flint, had been an officer and several N.C.O.s from each company. They had attended a short course of jungle training at the Far East Training Centre. They now began to teach the rest of the personnel the tactics which were to be used against the bandits in Malaya.

Weapon training, elementary jungle tactics and acclimatisation could be carried out satisfactorily on Singapore Island. But more was required to get the feel of the "real thing". So arrangements were made by the commanding officer, Lieutenant-Colonel Martyn,[1]

[1]Son of Brigadier-General A. Martyn, C.B., C.M.G., who commanded the 1st Battalion from March 1912 to October 1914.

THE 1ST BATTALION ON PARADE FOR INSPECTION BY THE COMMANDER-IN-CHIEF FARELF AT SINGAPORE. MARCH, 1954.

for two companies at a time to cross the Straits of Johore and train in an operational area on the mainland.

The Queen's Own moved up to their own operational area in Selangor, Malaya, by road and rail at the end of March. The operations carried out there against the Communist bandits are described in the next chapter.

★ ★ ★

The 1st Battalion returned to Singapore Island after three years in Malaya on February 25, 1954, and went again to Nee Soon Camp. Seven hectic days of handing in vehicles and equipment followed. There were no deficiencies. The Quartermaster and the M.T.O., Lieutenant Woolstencroft, could be proud of this feat. In fact, the report on the M.T. was "outstanding".

During the week at Nee Soon several officers visited the camp, including General Sir Charles Loewen, Commander-in-Chief Far East Land Forces (FARELF), who inspected the troops on the parade ground of the Malayan Basic Training Centre. Although they had seldom been on parade as a battalion for over three years, a high standard of drill was achieved. The Colours were carried by Lieutenant Stock and 2nd Lieutenant Nyren, a National Service officer. General Loewen was accompanied by Major H. B. H. Waring, his Military Assistant.

The British community went to considerable expense and trouble in entertaining all ranks during their short stay on the island.

The battalion embarked in the troopship "Empire Orwell" on March 3. At the docks many friends had assembled to say farewell. The following Queen's Own officers were there: Brigadier Talbot, who had flown from Malaya; Majors Gwilliam, H. B. H. Waring, Weymouth and Roper, who held Staff appointments in Singapore or Hong Kong; and Major Kemp, then serving with R.E.M.E. As the ship moved away, with the regimental flag at the masthead, the band of the 2nd/10th Gurkha Regiment played "A Hundred Pipers" and "Auld Lang Syne".

This time the Bay of Biscay was somewhat smoother, and the "Empire Orwell" reached Southampton on March 25, a day ahead of schedule. Brigadier Riddell, the Deputy Colonel of the Regiment, the advanced party and relatives and friends were on the quay. Two special trains took the troops to Maidstone, where the drums of the 4th/5th Battalion met them at the West Station. At Invicta Lines they dispersed on week-end leave.

On the morning of April 1 the battalion, with newly-arrived General Service Medals on their chests, marched through Maidstone with bayonets fixed. The route was Fairmeadow—High Street—Week Street and back to Invicta Lines. The salute was taken by the Mayor, Alderman T. Armstrong. The enthusiasm of the spectators was very moving. The decorations, especially those in Week Street, were magnificent. Having put away their rifles, the troops marched to a Civic Luncheon at the Royal Star Hotel. Six hundred and fifty strong, they were all seated in the ballroom when the Mayor arrived to a roar of "Kentish Fire". After toasts to Her Majesty The Queen and the Colonel-in-Chief, the Mayor proposed the health of the battalion. Lieutenant-Colonel Fyler, the commanding officer, replied. In the evening, the band and drums beat Retreat on the square of the Regimental Depot. They were watched by the Mayor, his councillors and the people of Maidstone. The day ended with a dance at the Royal Star Hotel, to which all ranks were invited.

Next morning the battalion was honoured by a visit from the Colonel-in-Chief at Invicta Lines. Captain Fletcher, from the Depot, acted as A.D.C. to Her Royal Highness. They arrived in a Land Rover lent by the 4th/5th Battalion. The Duchess was met by Lord Cornwallis, Lord Lieutenant of Kent, the Mayor of Maidstone and Brigadier Riddell. The parade was watched by members of The Past and Present Association and a number of relatives. After the inspection, the Colonel-in-Chief addressed the battalion. The march past was performed with precision. Some of the families who had been in Malaya were then presented to Her Royal Highness by Mrs. Fyler. The Duchess visited the sergeants' mess and lunched in the officers' mess before returning to London.

On April 3 the battalion went in a convoy of buses to Tonbridge. Having de-bussed at the Judd School, it marched through the town to the Castle with bayonets fixed. The salute was taken by Mrs. Salmon, Chairman of the Urban District Council. After an inspection on the Castle lawn, Mrs. Salmon addressed the troops. A Guard of Honour was provided by the 4th/5th. Also present were the standards of The Past and Present Association. Afterwards, the Tonbridge Council entertained the officers in the Council Chambers and the other ranks in the drill hall in Bank Street

THE 1ST BATTALION MARCHING THROUGH WEEK STREET, MAIDSTONE, 1ST APRIL, 1954.

THE 1ST BATTALION AT TONBRIDGE CASTLE, 3RD APRIL, 1954.

The next three months were occupied with leave and preparations for the move to Germany. A large number of experienced N.C.O.s and men left on discharge or re-posting. They were replaced by recruits. An unusually big advanced party had to be sent to Luneburg, the next station, to take over from The Royal Welch Fusiliers, who were vacating the barracks early. Indeed, before the end of June more than a third of the unit, under Major Grove, was at Luneburg. The remainder (less the band, which went to Shorncliffe) entrained at Maidstone West on June 28.

On the cold and wet evening of June 29, 1954, the main body arrived at Luneburg via Harwich and the Hook of Holland. As the train came into a siding, the pipes of the 1st Queen's Own Cameron Highlanders played "A Hundred Pipers". Then followed a fanfare by the trumpeters of The 8th King's Royal Irish Hussars, whose band played while the troops detrained and climbed into lorries. Also there was Brigadier J. F. M. MacDonald, who commanded the Lorried Infantry Brigade of the 7th Armoured Division, which the battalion was joining.

Luneburg is a pleasant market town, some 30 miles south of the port of Hamburg. Near it is the heath where Field-Marshal Montgomery accepted the unconditional surrender of the Germans in 1945. When the 1st Battalion arrived, the three barracks on the northern side of the town were occupied by The 8th Hussars, The Cameron Highlanders, an R.A.S.C. Lorry Company and a Field Ambulance. The Queen's Own were with Brigade Headquarters in Worcester Barracks on the southern side. Most of the married quarters, which were occupied by The Queen's Own families when they arrived in August, were close at hand. So were the training areas. In the town were a Y.M.C.A. establishment, a N.A.A.F.I. families' shop, clubs for officers and other ranks, and several good hostelries.

The battalion had arrived in the middle of the Rhine Army Collective Training Season, which in that year was more intense than any since the war. New tactical lessons had to be learned, and some old ones forgotten. That the troops rose successfully to the situation was no doubt due to the fact that, after their experience in Malaya, many of them were self-reliant, fit and used to operating in small groups. Such qualities were assets in a Lorried Infantry Brigade.

The first three months were spent almost entirely on the Soltau training area. Between exercises, Sevastopol Day was celebrated at Worcester Barracks on September 8. The Colonel of the Regiment came from Berlin and was present throughout the day. He took the salute at a march past after a drumhead service.

The Collective Training Season ended early in October. The final exercise, known as "Battle Royal", was a ten-day affair, in which all units of the Rhine Army took part. The object was to study tactical nuclear warfare on a large scale. As such, it was the first British exercise of its kind. The Queen's Own were in the van for five days and were on the move for the other five. The battalion worked with The 4th Queen's Own Hussars as its affiliated armoured regiment. The liaison between the two units was close.

In the winter the Rugby and hockey teams had successful tours in Berlin. The former beat the 1st Manchesters and the Berlin Wanderers but lost to the 1st Grenadier Guards. The latter won all its three matches, defeating a Berlin ex-international side, the 1st Royal Lincolnshire Regiment and the Berlin Independent Brigade.

The band rejoined from Shorncliffe in January 1955. From the day after its arrival it was kept busy playing at guest nights in the officers' mess, at all ranks' dances and weekly concerts in the N.A.A.F.I.

Colonel Fyler left to take command of the 130th Brigade (T.A.) in the South-West of England in February. He handed over to Major Flint, who commanded for a month until Lieutenant-Colonel Buckle arrived from England, where he had been on the Staff of the 56th (London) Armoured Division (T.A.).

The 1955 training season was another strenuous period. The Rhine Army was carrying out experiments with formation and unit organisations and with new weapons. Each company of the battalion was temporarily re-organised into four platoons, the personnel of the Mortar, Anti-Tank and Pioneer Platoons being attached as riflemen. The F.N. Automatic Rifle was issued for the season for user trials; training and shooting were done with that weapon.

Group training was carried out in June in the Soltau area. The battalion was affiliated to the 4th Royal Tank Regiment. They were together in camp for a month, during which a good team spirit was achieved. The cheerful log-fires in the evenings were long remembered. In a five-day brigade exercise, D Company made a night march behind the enemy lines and captured two tanks. In July three companies

THE COLONEL-IN-CHIEF INSPECTING THE 1ST BATTALION AT LUNEBURG, 7TH APRIL, 1956.

went to Schleswig-Holstein to act as enemy to the Danish Army; they enjoyed the change of scenery and the friendliness of the people. At the end of August the whole unit took part in a divisional exercise, after which it was praised for its realistic patrolling. This exercise included a night attack riding on tanks, and the defence of a village against an armoured assault. A large-scale manoeuvre, devised to test the experimental organisations, brought the season to a close. The Queen's Own acted as a motor battalion, each company being affiliated to a Tank squadron.

As a change from training, The Queen's Own provided 120 men, under Major Weymouth, to line part of the route on June 11, when H.R.H. The Duke of Edinburgh visited his regiment, The 8th Hussars. In August two teams, led by Lieutenant Tarver and 2nd Lieutenant Langhorne, took part in the Nijmegen marches in Holland. They completed the 100 miles course in four days without losing a point, and were awarded bronze medals. Also in August a three-day Battalion Rifle Meeting was held. The F.N. Rifle was used for some of the matches.

The Colonel-in-Chief visited the battalion at Luneburg on April 7, 1956. Captain Fletcher once more acted as A.D.C. to Her Royal Highness. Colonel Martyn, who was on the Staff of the Rhine Army at the time, represented the Colonel of the Regiment. As the Duchess walked slowly down the lines on her inspection of the parade, she stopped again and again to speak to men in the ranks. She then addressed the battalion. After the march past, Her Royal Highness drove to the officers' mess, where officers, their wives and local German dignitaries were presented to her and she took luncheon. Visits to the sergeants' and corporals' messes followed. There, non-commissioned officers and their wives were presented to her. As the Duchess drove away to Fassburg Aerodrome, cheering troops lined the route through the barracks.

The Queen's Own had some successes at sport in Germany. The Rugby football seven-a-side team won the divisional competition and was runner-up in the Rhine Army final. The cross-country runners had several minor victories.

Before the battalion left Luneburg Major-General G. Cooper, the commander of the 7th Armoured Division, wrote the following letter to Colonel Buckle: "I take this opportunity to thank you personally and your regiment. It has not only been an honour to have them under my command but a very great pleasure. You must be very proud of them . . . Ensure that they retain their individual action, which they displayed so well on manoeuvres and obviously in Malaya."

The main body left Luneburg in two trains early on June 8, 1956, the advanced party having gone on May 15. At the station to bid farewell were the band of the 1st Battalion The East Lancashire Regiment and representatives from all the neighbouring units. After a moderately smooth passage from the Hook, the troops were met at Harwich by the Colonel of the Regiment, the commander of the 3rd Infantry Division (Major-General J. B. Churcher) and the band of The King's Regiment. They went by rail to Dover.

4. *The 4th/5th Battalion (T.A.)*

At the beginning of 1951 the 4th/5th Battalion was disposed as follows: Battalion Headquarters and H.Q. Company at the T.A. Centre in Avebury Avenue, Tonbridge; the Support Company at the drill hall in Bank Street, Tonbridge; A Company at Maidstone; B Company at St. Mary Cray; C Company at Sevenoaks; and D Company at Penge, in the drill hall which had belonged to the former 5th Battalion. The 4th/5th was in the 133rd Brigade of the 44th (Home Counties) Division.

The Regular Permanent Staff consisted of an adjutant, a quartermaster, an R.S.M., six instructors (one for each company) and four rank and file. The rank and file were for the maintenance of vehicles, weapons and stores. The commanding officer was also a Regular.

The yearly compulsory training of personnel in the Territorial Army was much the same as it had been before the 1939-1945 War. Each officer and other rank had to perform a specified number of drills, according to whether he was a recruit or a trained soldier; he had to fire a weapon training course; and he had to attend annual camp for at least seven of the 14 days. All ranks who fulfilled their obligations received a Bounty. The sum of 2/6 was paid for each drill of two hours, in addition to travelling expenses to and from the drill hall.

With men still being called up for National Service, few young men enlisted into the Territorial Army. Most units were well under strength. So as to rectify this, the Army Council had decided that National Servicemen, on completion of their full-time service with the Regular Army, should go into the Territorial Army for three years. The first draft of National Servicemen had joined the 4th/5th in June 1950. Intakes had continued to arrive each fortnight until October. There was then a gap of six months. This was because the period of full-time National Service was extended from 18 months to two years owing to the war in Korea.

The 4th/5th, reinforced by drafts of National Servicemen, went to camp for its two weeks' annual training at the Western Heights. Dover, in June 1951 some 350 strong. At Bodney in 1952 the strength was over 400. By July 1953, when the camp was again at Bodney, the unit was practically up to strength. Most of the National Servicemen were from the 1st Battalion, then serving in Malaya.

The camps at Bodney were near the Practical Training Area at Stanford in Norfolk. This is a natural portion of the countryside some five miles by four. It is ideally suited to tactical training. The camps were mainly of huts, with all basic requirements but few amenities. The training, up to battalion level, was carried out under as near active service conditions as possible.

In 1951 and 1952 several borough and urban district councils in West Kent decided to implement the London and Home Counties scheme for fostering closer relations between the Territorial Army and Local Authorities by adopting companies of the 4th/5th Battalion. The dates on which the adoptions took place were:

Tonbridge—Battalion Headquarters, H.Q. Company and the Support Company on June 22, 1952.

Maidstone—A Company on March 8, 1952.

Orpington—B Company on May 21, 1951.

Sevenoaks—C Company on May 14, 1951.

Penge—D Company on April 26, 1951.

Bromley—D Company on January 25, 1951.

The adoption ceremony at Tonbridge was impressive. It took place on the lawn of the Castle before some 1,500 spectators. The parade, led by the drums wearing scarlet uniform, marched through the town to the Castle, where it was inspected by the Chairman of the Council, Mrs. E. M. Friend. After the inspection, illuminated addresses and plaques were exchanged.

When the Territorial Army was re-constituted in 1947, it had been intended that the former 5th Battalion The Queen's Own should become the divisional headquarters of the Royal Artillery of the 44th (Home Counties) Division at Bromley. The project had little success, since few recruits came in. So the Colonel of The Queen's Own had requested that the unit should be permitted to revert to an infantry role and be amalgamated with the 4th Battalion. Early in 1948 the Army Council had agreed to this; the Colours and most of the property of the former 5th Battalion had been moved from Bromley to Tonbridge. There the matter had rested, as Royal Assent was required before the amalgamation could be cemented. In 1952, under an Army Council Instruction dated May 2, Her Majesty Queen Elizabeth II was graciously pleased to approve of the new title "The 4th/5th Battalion The Queen's Own Royal West Kent Regiment".

When the 1st Battalion marched through Tonbridge in April 1954, the 4th/5th provided a Guard of Honour on the lawn of the Castle (See section 3 above). The guard was commanded by Major Meyrick. Lieutenant Ogilvie carried the Regimental Colour. The corps of drums was on parade.

The annual camp in June 1954 was at Ewshott, near Aldershot. Some of the men went to this Mecca of the Regular Army with some trepidation. Their fears were unfounded, for the battalion survived the fortnight with credit. The training was mainly a trial run for the divisional manoeuvres of the following year. It culminated in a strenuous brigade exercise. Socially, there were many compensations, for Aldershot, with its variety of entertainments, was within easy reach. Visitors included eight members of the councils of the towns which had adopted companies of the battalion.

In August, those who had been unable to attend annual training at Ewshott went to a small camp at Crowborough. In previous years the casuals had been attached to the Depot or to other units.

During the autumn, the Support Company moved from Tonbridge to a new drill hall in Speldhurst Road, Southborough.

For annual training in 1955 the 4th/5th went to a camp at

Tilshead. The tents were well laid out over a spacious area. The first week was spent in minor tactical training and a brigade exercise. Early on the second Sunday the battalion moved by road to a concentration area near Aldershot. From there, on the Tuesday, it went in lorries to Salisbury Plain, crossed the River Avon and advanced towards Warminster. The manoeuvres, in which tanks and aircraft co-operated, ended as the troops were attacking the final objective.

In order to economise, the Army Council then decided that the National Servicemen, although still liable to serve in the T.A. for three years, would only do one year's training of 20 days, including a camp. Later, it was announced that they would do no training at all. This decision meant that the National Servicemen would merely be paper strength, and that the number of men available for training would be drastically cut. Nevertheless, the 4th/5th Battalion entered 1956 with ambitious plans for the future.

CHAPTER 2

The First Battalion in Malaya

April 1951 — February 1954

1. *The Situation in Malaya*

DURING the early stages of the 1939-1945 War, the Malayan Communist Party, mostly Chinese, tried to obstruct the war effort. The German attack on Russia in June 1941 brought a reversal of this policy. Indeed, after the Japanese invasion of the Malayan Peninsula, the Party offered active help to the Malayan Government. Before the end of the war, the Malayan People's Anti-Japanese Army (M.P.A.J.A.) had come into being. This was a Communist-controlled organisation, which took to the jungle during the Japanese occupation. British personnel, with wireless sets and other equipment, were infiltrated into the country to act as liaison teams with the M.P.A.J.A.

When the Japanese surrendered in August 1945, the M.P.A.J.A. claimed that the victory was theirs and that they would now take charge. They kept much of the equipment brought to them by the British. Quantities of Japanese war material came into their hands. Their aim was the creation of a Malayan Communist People's Republic.

As Malaya settled down to post-war reconstruction, international Communism reared its head. In March 1948, a meeting of representatives of Asian Communist parties was held in Calcutta. From this conference it is suspected that orders came for an armed revolt in

MALAYA

AREA OF OPERATIONS OF THE FIRST BATTALION

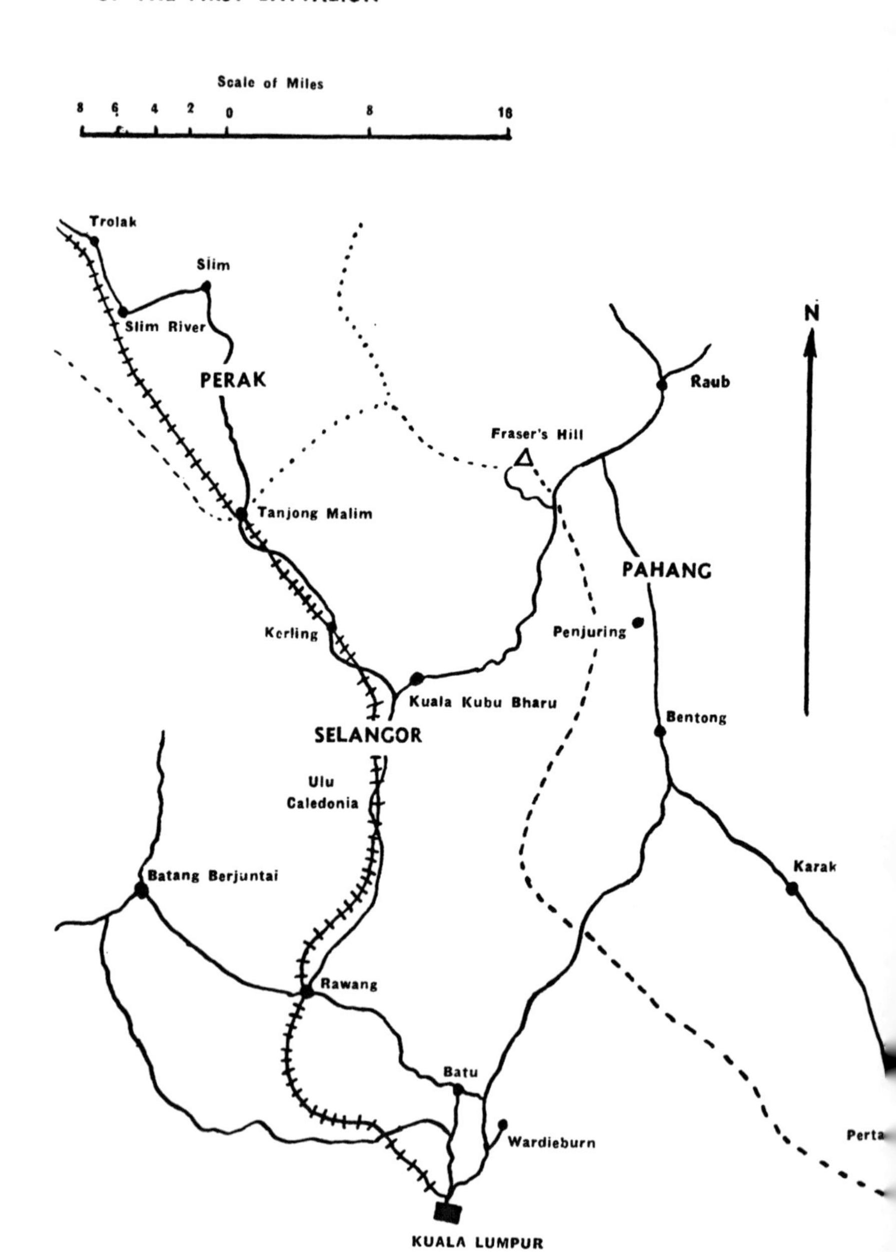

the Malayan Peninsula. Whether this is so or not, in June 1948 the units of the M.P.A.J.A. were mobilised again and terrorism began.

On June 16, three European planters were murdered in Perak by a gang of armed Chinese, who bound them and shot them with machine guns. Next day a State of Emergency was proclaimed in Perak and Johore. On the 18th, after a gang had attacked a Police Station in Johore, the Emergency was extended throughout the peninsula.

The Communist organisation again took to the jungle, where were hidden large quantities of arms and equipment against such an occasion. Its objects were to destroy the two basic industries of tin and rubber; to kill the mine and estate managers, together with all persons of all races who opposed the Communist attack; and to set up a so-called People's Republic.

The people—the Malays in particular—refused to join the Communists in overthrowing the Government. They rallied to its support, and took up arms in defence of their villages. The tin-miners and rubber-planters and their labour forces stood firm.

From the military point of view, the Communists had much in their favour. They had four or five thousand guerrillas in a country of which four-fifths is jungle, mountain and swamp. As long as they could get food and simple supplies from village shops, and as long as their ammunition lasted, they could hide and lay ambushes in the fringes of the jungle. Few of them wore uniform. A terrorist who buried his gun was not distinguishable from a rubber-tapper or any other worker.

By April 1951, the terrorist organisation was divided into the Malayan Races Liberation Army (M.R.L.A.) and the Min Yuen. The M.R.L.A. boasted a loose military organisation, the effectiveness of its sub-units depending very much on the calibre of the junior leaders. Armament normally consisted of grenades, pistols, carbines, rifles and a few light machine guns. The personnel usually wore khaki or jungle-green uniform with red-starred caps. They carried out the big ambushes and similar operations. The Min Yuen were everywhere; it was safe to trust nobody. They wore civilian clothes. They extorted money and food from the population; perpetrated political and other murders, often in a brutal fashion; collected information about the Security Forces, for example from agents in telephone exchanges; and generally supported the M.R.L.A.

In North Selangor, the part of Malaya with which we are concerned, there were three M.R.L.A. platoons—Nos. 8, 10 and 36. Their strength varied; when one was concentrated for an outrage it might mount to about 40. Nos. 8 and 10 were well-led, well-organised and well-armed, with at least two Bren guns each. No. 10 operated about Rawang. Against No. 8, as will be seen, The Queen's Own conducted a private war to the knife south of Kuala Kubu Bahru (K.K.B.). Farther north No. 36 did much sniping but, except for train derailments, was not so effective as the other two.

When the 1st Battalion The Queen's Own arrived, the campaign against the Communists was based on a plan made by General Sir Harold Briggs, the Director of Operations, who controlled all the Security Forces. The intention was to starve out the terrorists in the jungle by cutting them off from their food supplies, and then to kill them by barring their way in the jungle fringes. Much of their food was obtained from squatters, who lived in jungle clearings or open spaces near tin-mines and rubber-estates. These squatters were to be collected together in resettlement areas, thus being brought under control. Simultaneously, parts of the country were in turn to be made priority areas and were to be given "all-out treatment" by the Security Forces. The other areas were to be controlled by "framework" troops, whose task it was to eliminate as many terrorists as possible until their turn came.

The "framework" troops in Selangor were provided by the 18th Infantry Brigade, which consisted of the 1st Battalion The Suffolk Regiment, the 1st Battalion The Worcestershire Regiment and the 1st Battalion The Queen's Own. It was commanded by Brigadier R. T. K. Pye. Above Brigade the chain of command was through Headquarters South Malaya District (Major-General R. C. O. Hedley) to Headquarters Malaya (Major-General R. E. Urquart).

One of the essentials of the Briggs Plan was close co-operation between the Security Forces and the Federation Police. Technically the Army was in support of the Police, and relied on them greatly for information of all kinds. Each State was divided into Police Circles, which were sub-divided into Police Districts. Battalion and company commanders had to be hand-in-glove with the officers in charge of the Police Circles and Police Districts respectively; in fact, joint operation rooms were manned. In North Selangor, the headquarters of the Police Circle were at K.K.B. The headquarters of the

Police Districts were at Tanjong Malim in the north, K.K.B. in the centre and Rawang in the south.

2. Deployment of the 1st Battalion

The 1st Battalion The Queen's Own was deployed and fully operational in North Selangor by April 1, 1951. H.Q. Company was organised in the normal way, except for the scale of transport. This included a number of armoured three-ton vehicles; some trucks with armoured cabs; and ten armoured Humber scout cars, which had been converted for use as escort vehicles by the addition of twin Bren guns with magazines holding 100 rounds. The guns of the scout cars were manned by the corps of drums. The Rifle companies were organised on a patrol basis; a patrol consisted of ten men, divided into a Reconnaissance Group, the Commander, a Bren Group and a Reserve Group. Silent control was achieved in each patrol by hand signals. The Support Company was organised in the same manner as the Rifle companies, except for the three-inch Mortar Platoon, which carried out its usual task of support. No carriers were held.

At this stage the key personnel were:

Commanding Officer	Lieutenant-Colonel A. Martyn.
2nd-in-Command	Major D. H. Andrews, M.C.
Adjutant	Captain V. Dover, M.C.
Quartermaster	Captain A. E. Sivers, M.M.
R.S.M.	W.O.1 S. V. Stephens.
R.Q.M.S.	W.O.II J. E. Grubb.
O.C. H.Q. Company	Major G. P. Fawcett.
O.C. A Company	Major A. J. M. Flint, M.B.E.
O.C. B. Company	Major M. B. Rickcord.
O.C. C Company	Major P. E. Crook, O.B.E.
O.C. D Company	Major E. C. Spurr.
O.C. Support Company	Major P. C. M. Buckle.

A complete list of officers and warrant officers can be found in Appendix C.

Lack of men had as yet prevented D Company from being brought up to effective strength.

The operational area was from a point on the main trunk road 11 miles north of Kuala Lumpur (K.L.) to another point 70 miles farther north. In breadth it extended for 20 miles on either side of the road. The road was flanked for the most part by rubber-estates and, in the south, by tin-mines as well. Behind the estates and the mines was the jungle, into which the terrorists could always retreat. The bungalows of the planters and miners dotted the area between the road and the jungle on each side. They were usually in isolated positions on cleared mounds, surrounded by barbed-wire and guarded by special constables. They were good places from which to establish wireless communications.

On first deployment the battalion, less two companies, was in Erskine Camp at K.K.B., with A Company acting as "framework" troops in the southern part of the K.K.B. Police District and the Support Company in reserve. Erskine Camp consisted of *attap* huts, which were made of wood and rushes, had electric light, were cool and therefore suitable for the climate. B Company was on a rubber-estate at Kerling, where it was acting as "framework" troops in the northern part of the K.K.B. Police District. C Company was on another rubber-estate at Trolak as "framework" troops in the Tanjong Malim Police District. The two detached companies lived in tents and estate buildings, with camp structures. They each had transport, signallers and a mortar detachment under command. They had, too, their quota of Iban trackers from Borneo, 18 of whom were attached to the battalion. To act as interpreters with the trackers and the local population, a number of Junior Civilian Liaison Officers (J.C.L.O.s) were also attached. All three camps were protected by barbed-wire.

The "framework" troops in the Rawang Police District were provided by the 94th Squadron R.A.F. Regiment (Malaya), which was under command of the battalion. Colonel Martyn also normally had a Royal Armoured Corps Troop under his command for road patrol and escort duties. At first this was found by The 13th/18th Hussars, and later by The 12th Lancers.

Patrolling by each "framework" company was usually at the rate of two platoons out and one in camp. The latter guarded the camp and acted as stand-by platoon. Routine patrols might last from

ERSKINE CAMP. KUALA KUBU BAHRU, MALAYA.

A TYPICAL DETACHMENT CAMP IN MALAYA.

THE CORPS OF DRUMS OF THE 1ST BATTALION IN MALAYA, 1951.

24 hours to eight days, depending on the information available. Everything had to be carried, including hard rations. So, if a patrol were out for more than four days, it had to be maintained by air supply. Water was plentiful, but sterilising tablets had to be used when water-bottles were refilled. It was normal to move by day only, since operations were very difficult at night.

The country to be patrolled varied from rubber trees to virgin jungle. There were many water-courses, precipitous slopes, leeches, monkeys, insects and occasionally snakes. In the more difficult parts it was necessary to hack a way through the jungle; 500 yards to the hour was a fair rate of progress. Navigation was by map, compass and protractor, for visibility was restricted to a few yards. In fact, out on his own at night with little chance of wireless communication until the morning, a young patrol commander had to rely very much on himself.

On the administrative side, rations for the battalion had to be fetched all the way from K.L. four times a week and then distributed. This was a strain on vehicles and escorts, and the danger of ambushes was obvious. The chief problem was to give all ranks enough fresh food in the time allowed by the hot climate. Two-thirds of the troops were out on patrol at any one time and had to eat hard rations. It was necessary for their health to give them as much fresh food as possible when they returned to camp.

It was against this background that the 1st Battalion began its operations in North Selangor.

3. *Early Successes*

The first successful operation took place on the night of April 2. Acting on Police information, No. 1 Platoon of A Company under 2nd Lieutenant Beale laid an ambush on an estate in the southern part of the K.K.B. Police District. The platoon returned to Erskine Camp with the bodies of two uniformed terrorists, their rifles and ammunition.

On April 9, No. 2 Platoon of A Company laid an ambush on another estate in the same area. Two more bandits were killed.

On this occasion there was reason to suspect that more terrorists were lurking in the vicinity. So it was hastily surrounded before dawn by all available troops from K.K.B. On closing in, A Company found another dead bandit with his rifle. Two live terrorists were also seen but, as they were thought to be scouts, the cordon held its fire for the main body. Unfortunately there was no main body, and the affair ended with the departure of the "scouts" under a hail of belated bullets.

At the end of April, the Police were ambushed twice in the Rawang District. With the aid of a troop of Field Artillery and of the R.A.F., an assault was therefore made on the suspected area of jungle. No contact was made with the enemy. A few days later, two policemen were killed in a further ambush. After this, the Support Company was sent to garrison the area temporarily in order to raise morale and to dominate the terrorists there with mortar fire and patrols.

On May 16, acting on Police information, Nos. 5 and 6 Platoons of B Company from Kerling laid an ambush on an estate north of K.K.B. Three terrorists walked into the ambush and, in the words of Major Rickcord's signal, were "instantly destroyed". As well as their arms, over 7,000 Straits dollars (about £800) were recovered. One of the dead was a bandit of considerable notoriety.

C Company at Trolak had its first success on June 4, when No. 7 Platoon killed a bandit. This company had a very large district to patrol, and its camp was an unavoidably long way from its associated Police headquarters. So the success was a particularly fine effort, and the result of much hard work. In the affray, 2nd Lieutenant Howlett[1] had a lucky escape. A grenade landed at his feet but failed to explode.

Colonel Martyn had, on first deployment, decided to change companies over at two-monthly intervals. On June 1 the Support Company moved to Kerling, and B Company went into reserve at K.K.B. Two weeks later, A Company went to Trolak to relieve C Company, who became "framework" troops at K.K.B.

Meanwhile drafts of recruits had been arriving from England. Each draft on arrival had carried out jungle training under the 2nd-in-Command. From these drafts and their instructors, D Company had by June 26 been made up to strength. Captain Upton took

[1]Son of Brigadier B. Howlett, D.S.O. and Bar, of The Queen's Own, who was killed on the Sangro in November 1943.

command of it. Major Spurr, who should have commanded D Company, was performing the duties of the P.R.I.

This increase in strength enabled parties to be sent regularly on leave, usually to Penang.

Three changes took place in July and August. On July 20 the 94th Squadron R.A.F. Regiment ceased to be under command, and B Company moved from K.K.B. to take over at Rawang. On August 1 Major Fawcett became 2nd-in-Command vice Major Andrews, who had been posted to a first-grade Staff appointment at H.Q. Malaya. On August 21 the Support Company returned from Kerling to battalion reserve at K.K.B. on relief by the newly-formed D Company.

During these two months patrols were constantly locating vacant bandit camps, tracks, and dumps of food or stores. All of them were duly plotted in the operations room as part of the build-up of information. Two terrorists were killed, one by No. 9 Platoon of C Company near K.K.B. and one by No. 2 Platoon of A Company in the Trolak Forest Reserve. There were some "near misses" in the southern part of the K.K.B. Police District. In one of them a party of Police, which was investigating an incident, ran into No. 8 Platoon of the M.R.L.A. in strength. Although outnumbered, the Police charged, killing one bandit and capturing another. C Company was rushed to the scene, but a thunderstorm obliterated all tracks and no contact was made. The prisoner subsequently led patrols to several empty camps and food dumps.

On July 5 and 12 respectively Private Field and Lance-Corporal Pullen were wounded in engagements with bandits. The battalion had its first fatal casualty on August 22, when Private Hollebon died of wounds received in an action near Rawang. Corporal Bott was also wounded in this affair. They were members of a road patrol sent out by B Company. The patrol debussed when it came under automatic fire and counter-attacked by fire. In ensuing operations a further fleeting contact was made, but no known casualties were inflicted on the enemy.

For a very brave act on July 17, Private Searles of the Support Company was awarded a Bronze Medal and Certificate by the Royal Humane Society. He dived fully clothed and equipped into the flooded Selangor River and saved the life of his platoon commander, who had been swept away while leading an operational crossing.

An engagement was fought near Rawang by a party of B Company against No. 10 Platoon of the M.R.L.A. The result was inconclusive, but in a prolonged exchange of fire about 20 bandits were forced into precipitate flight by 2nd Lieutenant Wilson and four other ranks.

In September the Tanjong Malim Police District became the trouble area. Because of a raid by terrorists, which resulted in the death of two special constables, No. 11 Platoon of D Company was moved from Kerling to a temporary base near Tanjong Malim. On the 6th, while co-operating with A Company (Trolak), No. 11 Platoon was patrolling through overgrown rubber trees when it clashed with a gang of about ten bandits. The gang opened fire, wounding Lance-Corporal Wright and killing Private Elsley,[1] who was the leading scout. The platoon immediately attacked. The bandits withdrew, with no known casualties. In the follow-up operations No. 11 Platoon exacted some retribution by killing a member of the gang. On the 28th, No. 1 Platoon of A Company ambushed and killed two terrorists near Slim village. On October 4, No. 10 Platoon of D Company killed another near Tanjong Malim.

There were more successes in other parts of the operational area, and with 18 terrorists to its credit in the first six months, the battalion could look back on an excellent start.

September ended with a tragic battle accident, in which Corporal Henderson died of wounds and Private York and an Iban tracker were injured. Henderson had joined the regiment as a boy in 1935; he had served with the 2nd Battalion in Malta and Leros during the war.

4. *The Ambush on the Ulu Caledonia Estate*

October 1951 was a grim month for The Queen's Own. It began with the death of Sir Henry Gurney, the High Commissioner in Malaya. On the evening of the 6th Colonel Martyn, on his return to K.K.B. from a 24 hours' operation, was greeted with the shattering news that Sir Henry had been ambushed and killed soon after mid-day

[1]Private Elsley's parent regiment was The East Surrey Regiment. Many of the personnel serving with the 1st Battalion belonged to different regiments of the Home Counties Brigade.

A TYPICAL SOLDIER OF THE 1ST BATTALION ON PATROL IN MALAYA, 1951.

on the Fraser's Hill road. This road ran north-eastwards over a mountain range from K.K.B. to Raub in the State of Pahang. The scene of the ambush was a steep bend about a mile short of the battalion boundary. No one in the unit or at Brigade H.Q. knew of the journey Sir Henry was making that day.

In a hurried conversation with Brigadier Pye, Colonel Martyn was ordered to take command of the pursuit with all of his own troops who could be made available, and two companies of The Worcestershire Regiment who were moving up to come under command. The 2nd/2nd Gurkha Rifles and the R.A.F. were to co-operate.

Battalion Tactical Headquarters moved out from Erskine Camp for the scene of the ambush within half an hour. Orders were left for C Company, the Support Company and the two Worcestershire companies to follow to a forward rendezvous as soon as possible.

It was pitch dark by the time that the 20 miles of winding mountainous road had been climbed. Already on the scene were the attached troop of The 13th/18th Hussars and the stand-by platoon from K.K.B. Colonel Martyn was told that a gang of some 40 bandits with light machine guns had evidently crossed the battalion boundary from Pahang to lay the ambush. The culprits were, in consequence, almost certain to have withdrawn into the thick jungle of Pahang, which neither The Queen's Own nor The Worcestershires knew. It was because the wireless vehicle of Sir Henry Gurney's police escort had broken down that news of the outrage had been slow in coming through. There was no hope of movement off the road until dawn, but a cordon could be placed round the most likely area.

During the night a cordon, consisting of the Support Company, the two Worcestershire companies and a detachment of the 2nd/2nd Gurkha Rifles, was sent out along the roads surrounding an extensive area. At dawn on the 7th, C Company moved in on the tracks of the terrorists. The R.A.F. arranged an air blockade to close the many unavoidable gaps in the cordon, and bombed particularly suspected places. Some gunners shelled other likely targets. The Hussars patrolled the roads continuously. But, although C Company found several large empty camps, no terrorists were found.

The commander of the 48th Brigade in Pahang, having set up his Tactical Headquarters at Raub, then assumed control of the operations The area of search was changed. While two Queen's Own companies and one Worcestershire company threw a cordon round it, the 2nd/2nd Gurkha Rifles moved across it in five columns. Again no contact was made. So the search was switched to another area deeper in Pahang, and The Queen's Own returned to camp, having been out for ten days.

The Gurkhas kept up the pressure for the best part of six weeks. They accounted for six terrorists, who probably belonged to the gang which had killed Sir Henry Gurney.

★ ★ ★

The 1st Battalion had resumed its routine operational duties by October 20. On that day, No. 11 Platoon of D Company was on a 48 hours' patrol on the Ulu Caledonia Estate, near the southern edge of the K.K.B. Police District. On the morning of the 22nd this platoon, having completed its task, assembled at its rendezvous at the estate buildings. There it was picked up by transport, which had been brought out from Kerling by Captain Deed. The return journey started at about ten o'clock, with a three-ton lorry in the lead, followed by a 15-cwt truck and a scout car. The estate track ran through rubber trees and undergrowth, intersected by irrigation ditches.

When the convoy had gone about two miles towards the trunk road, some kind of bomb was detonated under the three-ton lorry. Then the personnel in the lorry came under fire from some 40 terrorists, who were concealed in ditches on two steep hillocks to the right. Two Bren guns and a Japanese heavy machine gun were in action, as well as rifles and carbines. Captain Deed, Corporal Sulley (who was acting as Platoon Sergeant) and three others in the lorry were killed by the first bursts. The Platoon Commander, 2nd Lieutenant Gregson, was seriously wounded. Within a few moments Lance-Corporal Martin was the only officer or N.C.O. in the lorry alive and uninjured. He assumed command. The truck and the scout car, which had just turned a corner, stopped. The rank and file in the truck jumped out and took cover. The twin Bren guns of the scout car opened fire, but were soon put out of action by a hit on the mounting.

This was a situation to test the highest courage. The men of No. 11 Platoon were not found wanting. They took up positions under the vehicles or in the shelter of a bank on the right and fought back. The bandits, unable to subdue the troops by fire, rolled grenades down from the hillocks on to the track and resorted to weird yells and calls to surrender. Lance-Corporal Martin was badly wounded. Private Pannell, a Regular soldier, took command. By moving from place to place with a fine disregard for his own safety, he inspired the others to beat back all attempts of the enemy to charge. After about an hour the terrorists withdrew, leaving three of their weapons behind. If that thin jungle-green line had given way, five Bren guns as well as the normal complement of rifles and carbines of a platoon could have fallen into hostile hands. That would have been a disaster of the first magnitude. By its staunch resistance, No. 11 Platoon had upheld the tradition of The Queen's Own not to yield whatever the odds.

After the terrorists had gone Private Pannell, who had been hit four times, and Lance-Corporal Parish, a signaller who had been in the truck, walked back along the track to the estate buildings to telephone for help. But the line had been cut by the shooting.

While the fight had been going on the Estate Manager, Mr. Pearse, had driven into the midst of it in an armoured car. His driver had been killed. Of the four special constables with him, one had been killed and three wounded. After the action, his vehicle was backed out by the driver of the lorry, Private New, who had miraculously not been hit. It was by this means that the news of the ambush was first made known.

When the news reached Erskine Camp, the call for the stand-by platoon was sounded on the bugle. This platoon (the Machine Gun Platoon, commanded by Lieutenant Fletcher) set out without delay. Having debussed on the trunk road, it doubled up the winding track which led to the Ulu Caledonia Estate. As it did so. a sustained tropical downpour began. This rain obliterated traces of the terrorists, thus hampering the follow-up operations.

When Lieutenant Fletcher's platoon arrived, the signs of the desperate struggle were still visible. The lorry, the truck and the scout car were spaced over some 100 yards of the track. All three vehicles had punctured tyres and smashed windscreens. The lorry and the truck were riddled with bullets. In the lorry and in positions, from which they had been firing, were one officer, ten other ranks and three Iban trackers dead. Nearby were one officer, ten other ranks and one J.C.L.O. wounded. Those who could walk or hop had done what they could to make the more seriously injured comfortable and to drag them under the vehicles out of the rain. Lying among the casualties were four dead terrorists, who had been shot as they tried to charge.

The names of the dead can be found in the Roll of Honour. Besides 2nd Lieutenant Gregson, Lance-Corporal Martin and Private Pannell, the wounded were: Privates Atkins, Cheeseman R., Clements, Harman, Lepper, Perkins, Wheatstone, Wheeler and Wickins and J.C.L.O. Chan. The only unwounded men were Lance-Corporal Parish, Private New, and Drummer Butcher and Private Pope, the gunner and the driver of the scout car. Private Lepper, whose wound was in the abdomen, died in hospital two days later.

For their gallantry in this fight, Private Pannell and Lance-Corporal Martin received immediate awards of the D.C.M. and M.M. respectively; Drummer Butcher and Lance-Corporal Parish were mentioned in despatches; and Private Wheeler received a Commander-in-Chief's Certificate.

While the two Bren groups of Lieutenant Fletcher's platoon went to picquet the hillocks, the remainder rendered first aid to the wounded. The medical officer, ambulances and the rest of the Support Company were summoned by wireless from K.K.B. Before they came, a terrorist was seen crawling away through the undergrowth. He failed to answer the call to surrender and was shot.

When the reinforcements arrived from K.K.B., the Support Company protected the medical officer (Captain Davidson, R.A.M.C.) while he tended the wounded, assisted in the evacuation of the dead, and reconnoitred for traces that would help the follow-up operations. In the process, a terrorist was found hiding in a thicket. He too refused to surrender and was killed.

Darkness was closing in before orders for the follow-up operations had been completed. C Company from K.K.B. was sent to make a quick drive through jungle close to the Ulu Caledonia Estate. Several crossing places on the trunk road were picqueted. No contacts were made. At dawn a cordon was thrown round an area, which knowledge of the bandits' habits had shown to be promising. For the next ten days many square miles of country were cordoned and searched by sectors. Although subsequent information revealed that the troops were on the right track, there was no immediate result. Two companies of the 1st Battalion The Suffolk Regiment were put under command for these operations, and the R.A.F. co-operated by bombing large areas of jungle. No friends could have been more eager to help The Queen's Own to avenge their grievous losses.

5. *Five Successful Months*

After that sombre October, the battalion increased its efforts. Many successes were achieved. There were some setbacks. Only the more important events will be recorded.

On November 26 the Pioneer Platoon (Lieutenant Norton), which was stand-by platoon at Erskine Camp, was sent out to investigate an incident. It was ambushed at the $44\frac{3}{4}$ milestone on the trunk road, about six miles north of K.K.B. Privates Burford, Clark, Everset, Hills and Mann were slightly wounded. Having jumped from its vehicles, the platoon returned the fire and then charged. As usual the terrorists fled. The pioneers pursued them in extended order through scrub. In the pursuit Private Holman, a stretcher-bearer, was killed. There was a good deal of shooting and confusion at the time, and what had happened was not immediately apparent. Holman's rifle and ammunition were lost. The rifle was recovered in March 1953, as will be seen.

Another ambush occurred at this place on the night of March 29, 1952. There were no casualties. But Private Pankhurst of the Support Company had a narrow escape. For the $44\frac{3}{4}$ milestone, which he was using as cover, had a piece of concrete the size of a saucer knocked out of it by a bullet. Before the battalion left Malaya, the officers of the K.K.B. Police Circle presented a silver replica of the milestone to the officers of The Queen's Own as a memento of this spot. The real stone was brought home to England and was erected outside the Maidstone Museum.

Lieutenant Norton and Private Murrell were wounded on December 11, 1951, while the Support Company was operating with the 1st Battalion The Suffolk Regiment near K.L.

A week later, D Company moved from Kerling to a new camp just south of Tanjong Malim. The change was necessary because there had been a serious deterioration in the situation in the Tanjong Malim Police District, where the terrorists were dominating the labour force on the estates and work was virtually at a standstill. The rapid construction of this new camp on virgin soil was typical of the Quartermaster and his staff. Indeed, their efficiency was a basic factor in everything the battalion achieved.

The Christmas festivities were spaced over Christmas Eve, Christmas Day and Boxing Day so that a proper state of readiness could be maintained. In the circumstances, all ranks had a reasonably good time. Many of the married personnel were able to spend at least one of the days with their families, who had arrived and were living at the "family station" in K.L. A number of other ranks were entertained at a lavish party given by European civilians at the K.K.B. Club. Some of the officers, who went on leave to Singapore, owed much to Brigadier C. H. McVittie (the Director of Ordnance Services, FARELF, and formerly of The Queen's Own) and his wife, whose house they used as a veritable transit camp. A bountiful supply of toffees for all ranks and the families was received from Edward Sharp and Sons Ltd. of Maidstone, who sent similar generous gifts each Christmas the battalion was overseas.[1]

Lieutenant-Colonel A. Martyn, O.B.E., completed his period of command on January 19, 1952, and handed over to Lieutenant-Colonel G. G. Elliott, D.S.O. He became A.Q.M.G. at the headquarters of FARELF in Singapore.

When the change of commanding officers took place, the number of bandits killed was 38. It was raised two days later to 41 by D Company, who were having a run of successes near Tanjong Malim. These three terrorists were killed in an ambush laid by Corporal Healey's section. Follow-up operations were carried out by six platoons, but were not successful.

Pressure was increased in February, mainly against No. 8 Platoon of the M.R.L.A. During the third week of that month, ten terrorists were accounted for, the highest weekly total so far. This included five who were killed by No. 7 Platoon of C Company. The story of this fine small action, for which 2nd Lieutenant Howlett received an immediate award of the M.C., follows:

On the afternoon of February 21, No. 7 Platoon left K.K.B. to destroy a bandit camp. The platoon, which was some 20 strong, went

[1]This famous West Kent firm sent gifts on other occasions, including Easter Eggs.

in transport to the Ulu Caledonia Estate. Thence it was guided through jungle by a member of the Min Yuen, who had surrendered. Having moved carefully for a few miles, No. 7 Platoon lay up for the night. Next morning it went on, crawling at times to avoid being seen by the rubber-tappers. The bandit camp was found, but the occupants had gone, leaving behind some documents and equipment. The platoon started back by another route. As the leading scout, Private Manktelow, emerged from the jungle on to the estate, he reported that he could see five armed, khaki-clad bandits walking along a track about 100 yards away. 2nd Lieutenant Howlett made a quick plan. He sent No. 2 Section on to high ground to the left, and ordered the Platoon Headquarters Group to give covering fire. He himself led No. 1 Section in a direct attack. The bandits, alternately moving and firing, tried to escape. No. 1 Section gave chase. One terrorist was shot dead by the Platoon H.Q. Group. The other four ran off through the undergrowth until they became exhausted. Two got into a ditch and opened fire: they were killed by a grenade thrown by Howlett. Another was wounded and hid in a hole, where he was killed by a grenade also thrown by Howlett. The fifth bandit ran up a hill. He was hunted down and shot by 2nd Lieutenant Elwell and five men. The area was then searched, and four rifles and a grenade were found.

The Min Yuen renegade, who had acted as guide, said that two of these five terrorists had taken part in the ambush of No. 11 Platoon on the Ulu Caledonia Estate the previous October. He also said that No. 8 Platoon of the M.R.L.A. was in a bad way. This apparently was true. For after numerous food dumps had been destroyed near Rawang, incidents in the area became few and far between. Before the end of March, No. 8 Platoon of the M.R.L.A. had ceased to be a serious menace. The Ulu Caledonia ambush had been avenged.

Routine operations were suddenly interrupted on March 25 by an ambush carried out by No. 36 Platoon of the M.R.L.A. just outside Tanjong Malim. At about 7.30 in the morning the Support Company, the "framework" troops there at the time, heard firing from the north-east. Major Buckle telephoned the Police District Headquarters and was told that the Assistant District Police Officer, the civil engineer and a Malay police squad had gone out to investigate a break in the town's water pipe-line; it was feared that they had been ambushed. The Machine Gun Platoon was on the move within ten minutes.

When it reached the pipe-line, firing had ceased and the bandits had fled northwards. The Police officer, the engineer and most of the squad were dead. Blood tracks were followed, but they soon faded out. Even the Iban trackers lost the trail. Air strikes were called for. Although they were put down promptly on the terrorists' escape route, the gang got away.

After this outrage, Colonel Elliott was ordered to move his Tactical Headquarters and his reserve company to Slim River and to help to form a new Police District in South Perak. This meant that the battalion was split asunder, with B, D and the Support Companies in South Perak under the 3rd Commando Brigade, and A and C Companies still under the 18th Brigade in North Selangor.

The battalion had its 17th fatal battle casualty on April 10, when Private Lowday was killed on operations. Up till then, 55 terrorists had been killed by The Queen's Own.

6. *Rest and Re-training*

The Queen's Own handed over their commitments on April 17, 1952, to the 2nd/2nd Gurkha Rifles in the north and to the 1st Suffolk in the south. On the same day the battalion, less two companies, moved by road to Wardieburn Camp near K.L. A freak storm had blown down a number of the huts, so that there was not enough accommodation for the whole unit. So, on the 21st, B and C Companies went from Trolak and Rawang respectively by train and ferry to Penang, where they occupied Minden Barracks. A month later A, D and the Support Companies changed over with B and C.

The battalion was free of jungle operations for two months for rest and re-training. The aims in order of priority were: refit, re-train, rest, recreation. After more than a year on operations, all of these were badly needed. The standard of fieldcraft and of shooting had fallen off, mainly owing to the continual turnover of personnel. No less than 23 officers had gone since the unit had arrived in Malaya; 19 had joined. Moreover, the battalion was five sergeants and 23 corporals short of establishment, so that numerous new N.C.O.s had to be trained.

As part of re-training, much use was made of the Batu Caves Rifle Range near K.L. A very successful Battalion Rifle Meeting was held there. This was probably the reason why The Queen's Own did so well in the Malayan Rifle Meeting, which took place at Port Dickson at the end of July. The team, trained by Major Buckle, won the Unit Championship by seven points. It also won the Rifle and the Light Machine Gun Team Championships.

Two weeks before the battalion resumed jungle operations General Sir Gerald Templer, the new High Commissioner in Malaya, was the principal guest at a dinner in the officers' mess at Wardieburn Camp.

7. *Re-deployment*

When the 1st Battalion resumed operations on June 17, 1952, Headquarters returned to K.K.B., with B Company acting as "framework" troops and the Support Company in reserve. D Company was at Rawang. A Company went to Batang Berjuntai in the Selangor Coast Police Circle. C Company, the band and the administrative details remained at Wardieburn Camp in the Selangor Central Police Circle. Control and administration were difficult, because Battalion Headquarters was at the northern extremity of the operational area and the administrative base was at the southern end.

The area was extraordinarily quiet. Arduous patrolling brought little profit. This was satisfactory for the peaceful-minded, but disappointing for the blood-thirsty. D Company did in fact kill one terrorist and wound another on June 26; one bandit surrendered. A few days later No. 8 Platoon of C Company killed a terrorist just north of K.L.

The Queen's Own had by now received about half of the war-dogs in Malaya. They were of two types—attacker and tracker. The former were a mixed blessing, since they were unable to distinguish between friend and foe unless they were carefully pointed at a target. The trackers were most useful as guard dogs, since they gave warning of any hostile approach. They replaced many sentries, thus giving the men more sleep. To start with, they were not so physically fit as the patrols they accompanied. It was unfortunate that the area was so quiet, as they could not be given a fair trial.

In July the detachment at Batang Berjuntai was reduced to one platoon. The rest of A Company was withdrawn into reserve at K.K.B. The Support Company (less the Mortar Platoon, which remained operational) became a training cadre temporarily, the personnel being distributed among the four Rifle companies. Even so, the strength of the battalion had fallen so low that these companies were on an average only 70 strong.

By the end of July the police jungle squads and the special constables had been reorganised. Having received more training, they were able to take over increasingly the responsibility for routine patrolling of the rubber-estates and even for ambushes. The troops went deeper into the jungle, supporting the police only when necessary. Their role gradually changed from patrolling to duties in aid of the civil power.

Private Denton was killed on September 11 while he was on operations with No. 5 Platoon of B Company.

As already mentioned in the first section of Chapter I, the battalion was honoured by a visit from the Colonel-in-Chief and her elder son, The Duke of Kent, at K.K.B. on October 7. Because heavy rain had made the *padang* unfit the battalion, less C and D Companies, was formed up on the road in front of the officers' mess at Erskine Camp. The inspection took longer than had been expected for, as Her Royal Highness said: "These are my soldiers and I have come a long way to see them." After the inspection, the Duchess addressed the troops on parade. She then visited the sergeants' mess and lunched with the officers, whose wives had driven out from K.L. for the occasion. There was a special programme for the Duke, including demonstrations by the war-dogs, and he fired an Owen gun on the 30 yards range. In the afternoon, Her Royal Highness received a number of junior N.C.O.s and privates in the corporals' club. After spending nearly four hours at K.K.B., the Royal party left for K.L. There the Duchess had tea in the Wives' Club, and Mrs. Elliott presented most of the other ranks' wives to her. While they were in K.L. the Colonel-in-Chief and her son stayed at King's House, the guard over which was provided by C Company.

Operationally there was little excitement. A few terrorists were killed, but information about their movements was difficult to obtain. Efforts were increased to starve them out in the jungle, thus forcing them to emerge for food. In addition to frequent searches and sealing

THE COLONEL-IN-CHIEF ADDRESSING THE 1ST BATTALION AT K.K.B., 7TH OCTOBER, 1952.

THE COLONEL-IN-CHIEF TAKES THE SALUTE AT K.K.B., 7TH OCTOBER, 1952.

off of villages, expeditions were sent deep into the jungle to destroy vegetables, which were being grown in clearings.

An example of the expeditions into the jungle was that carried out by C Company under Captain Abplanalp. This company went out from Wardieburn Camp to destroy crops in 11 large clearings, which had been located from the air. After two days' march through thick and hilly jungle, a base camp was established. Thence, patrols were sent to find the clearings and destroy the vegetables. Except for the first three days' rations, the troops were supplied entirely by air drops. The company returned after three weeks, having destroyed the crops in eight clearings.

In an attack on a bandit camp on November 6 by No. 11 Platoon of D Company, Private Latter was killed.

At about this time, Captain Wilton and Staff-Sergeant Thompson of the Royal Army Pay Corps arrived to establish a Central Battalion Pay Office, the first to be set up overseas. It relieved the P.R.I., the company commanders and the colour-sergeants of much paper work.

A hall, known as the Sevastopol Cinema, was constructed in Erskine Camp in time for Christmas. All kinds of entertainments were held in it, including those given by touring companies from England, such as the Carole Carr and the Brian Reece Shows.

For Christmas, the Planters' Association gave a generous gift of 1,100 dollars. *The Daily Express* sent a bottle of beer, chocolate and cigarettes for every man. Four cases of books and 100 parcels came from "The Comforts for Korea and Malaya Fund". Among the Christmas parties organised for the troops were those at the K.K.B. Club and the Lake Club in K.L.

Just before Christmas Lieutenant-Colonel Elliott, who had already had one spell in hospital, was again on the sick list. He was flown home to England at short notice. Major Buckle assumed command until March 8, 1953, when Lieutenant-Colonel A. R. Fyler[1] arrived from a Staff appointment in Hong Kong to take over.

In the New Year, Major Buckle began a series of operations near K.K.B. The intention was to force the terrorists in the locality to surrender by making the collection of food even more difficult. The

[1]Great nephew of Colonel A. E. Fyler, who commanded the 1st Battalion from 1881 to 1883, and wrote "The History of The 50th (The Queen's Own) Regiment."

R.A.F. dropped bombs into the jungle by night as well as by day. A troop of 25-pounders, assisted by mortars and medium machine guns, harassed selected areas. This went on for nearly two weeks, while patrols lay in ambush waiting for the bandits to emerge from their hides. Success came on February 2. Information had been received that some terrorists were meeting rubber-tappers to the east of the trunk road just south of K.K.B. By dawn two companies and some police patrols had cordoned the area. C Company, led by Major Waring, then swept through it. One bandit was killed and another was wounded and captured. The wounded man was willing to give information.

After the informer had left hospital, he led patrols to food dumps and indicated places for ambushes. As a result, large quantities of food were discovered and nine terrorists were killed in a month. Two of the nine were shot on March 3 by a patrol commanded by Sergeant Vine; one of the bandits killed in this clash was carrying the rifle which had been lost by the Pioneer Platoon in November 1951. These achievements virtually put a stop to terrorist activity in the vicinity of K.K.B.

One of the *attap* huts in Erskine Camp was converted by the pioneers into a chapel, wherein services were conducted by the padre, the Rev. T. James. All Saints' Chapel, as it was named, became the place of worship for the European Community of K.K.B. as well as the troops. It was dedicated on April 12 by the Rev. E. C. W. Knight, the Deputy Assistant Chaplain-General, in the presence of Major-General Sir Hugh Stockwell, G.O.C. Malaya, and of the Colonel of the Regiment, who had recently assumed the appointment of Principal Staff Officer to the High Commissioner and was stationed in K.L.

In April, Colonel Fyler was appointed to command the Security Forces in the K.L. area in an operation known as "Maze". He moved with his Tactical Headquarters to the High Street Police Station in K.L., where a combined military and police operations room was established. He had under his command a small Police Field Force, one company of The Somerset Light Infantry and A, B and D Companies of The Queen's Own. A Company (Major Bishop) was based at Wardieburn Camp. B Company (Major Archer) and D Company (Major Upton) were accommodated in camps about ten miles from K.L. The rest of the battalion remained in North Selangor, with Headquarter Company (Major Faulkner) and C

EXTERIOR OF ALL SAINTS' CHAPEL, K.K.B.

INTERIOR OF ALL SAINTS' CHAPEL, K K.B.

Company (Major Waring) based on Erskine Camp, and the Support Company (Major Roper) on Rawang. With this smaller force, Major Buckle started another operation called "Sting".

The main object of the two operations was to cut off the bandits from their food supplies. During them, B Company discovered a large dump of arms; C Company found an occupied camp and wounded two terrorists and captured ten packs containing important documents; the Support Company ambushed and shot two terrorists; and D Company had a fatal casualty, 2nd Lieutenant Manning being killed on April 23.

Acting on information, the Special Branch of the Police organised a raid on a squatter area in the outskirts of K.L. on June 16. Twelve policemen set out at dawn; Colonel Fyler and his Intelligence Officer, Lieutenant Leigh,[1] went with them. Five bandits were found hiding in a well. Two jumped out after each had thrown a grenade. The first grenade exploded, and one bandit got away. The second grenade came to rest only a yard from Lieutenant Leigh who, regardless of his own safety, rose to his feet and shot the second bandit as he rushed at him. That grenade failed to detonate. The other three terrorists were forced out of the well by tear gas and were captured. During a search which followed, a sixth bandit was discovered in a grave, which was covered by planks with earth on top of them, air being provided by a long wooden pipe.

On Coronation Day, June 2, the battalion had three detachments on parade besides the contingent in London. At K.L. 14 other ranks under Captain Abplanalp took part in a colourful parade on the *padang,* in which the Royal Navy and the Royal Air Force as well as Army units were represented. At K.K.B. Major Buckle commanded a parade which included Boy Scouts, Girl Guides, Police, Sakai with their blowpipes, and a detachment of The Queen's Own under Major Waring. At Rawang the Support Company provided a contingent for a smaller parade, which was commanded by Major Roper.

When the Coronation contingent returned from London, it brought with it the Victoria Cross and medals won by Sergeant Coleman in the Crimea and the Indian Mutiny. They had been purchased as a memorial to the members of the battalion who lost their lives in Malaya. The names of those who had up till then lost their lives

[1]Son of Major J. T. Leigh of The Queen's Own.

in Malaya were inscribed on a Memorial Tablet, which was placed in All Saints' Chapel at K.K.B.[1] The money for the decoration, medals and tablet was obtained from a raffle and by contributions from all ranks. The names of those who contributed were written in a Memorial Book.

Soon after the Coronation Colonel Fyler, his Tactical Headquarters and B Company moved back to K.K.B. from K.L. The officer commanding the 1st Somerset Light Infantry became responsible for "Maze". In operations under him on July 1, Private Stevenson of A Company was killed when a food-container, which had been dropped from the air, fell on him after being entangled in a tree.

In August Colonel Fyler was told that the battalion was to move soon to Bentong in Pahang. Most of the troops were glad to hear this, since it was becoming increasingly difficult to locate terrorists in North Selangor. Bentong was known to be a good area for finding them.

During a farewell party in the officers' mess at K.K.B. on September 26, information came in that a bandit camp had been seen near Kerling. Major Waring took out Nos. 7 and 8 Platoons of C Company to attack it. One terrorist was shot in the assault, which was led by 2nd Lieut. Neve.[2] Three more were killed by the cordon troops under Lieutenant Lygo. This brought the total of bandits killed by the battalion to 85.

A farewell parade was held at K.K.B. on October 3. The troops marched through the town with Colours flying and the band and drums at their head. The salute was taken by the District Officer who, on behalf of the Malayan people in North Selangor, presented to the Queen's Own a shield on which was depicted a map of Malaya in silver.

Just before the move to Bentong, Brigadier Talbot arrived to take command of the 18th Brigade.

8. *Bentong*

The move to Pahang was accomplished by road at the end of

[1] When the emergency ended in 1960, the camp at K.K.B. was handed over to a Malayan unit and this tablet was brought home to the Regimental Headquarters at Maidstone.

[2] Son of Major G. E. Neve (See page 10).

October 1953. Battalion Headquarters, Headquarter Company and C Company were at Bentong; A Company was at Sungei Pertang; B Company at Karak; D and the Support Companies were at Sungei Penjuring. At all four camps the accommodation was mainly in aged tents. A and B Companies were short of water, while a water-borne stomach disease nearly got a grip on the troops at Sungei Penjuring.

In Pahang there were fewer rubber-estates but larger areas of jungle than in Selangor. Lengthy operations away from camp became more frequent. Much use was made of helicopters, both for reconnaissance and for dropping supplies. The troops quickly adapted themselves to these new conditions. Before long the battalion was killing, on an average, more than one bandit each week.

2nd Lieutenants Follett-Smith and Morley-Jacob, who had only arrived in the country in September, were responsible for a notable operation. They took out Nos. 2 and 3 Platoons of A Company and managed to surround a bandit camp silently in spite of a swarm of hornets. The three occupants of the camp were killed. Private Sanggau, an Iban tracker, shot two of them with one bullet as they rushed at him, one being killed outright and the other being finished off by Sanggau with his *parang*.

Four platoons under Major Crumplin spent Christmas and the New Year festival in the jungle. The platoons were: No. 1 (Lieutenant Wood), No. 8 (2nd Lieutenant Neve), No. 9 (2nd Lieutenant Fraser) and No. 10 (2nd Lieutenant Newall).[1] The object was to destroy crops in several clearings, which had been seen from the air. Using the first clearing that was located as a base for the expedition, Major Crumplin divided his force into two columns. They found six other clearings, destroyed the crops in them and killed four terrorists. The force returned after 21 days, having been supplied for 17 of them by air-drops. Six sick men had been evacuated by helicopters. A few days later Nos. 8 and 10 Platoons, led by 2nd Lieutenant Neve, went back to the same area and killed three bandits, who had re-occupied the clearings.

Two important terrorists were killed on January 25 in a clever night ambush laid by Corporal Ball of D Company. This brought the battalion's total to 106, which was exceeded by only three other units.

[1]Son of Lieutenant-Colonel E. J. Newall, who served in The Queen's Own, 1923-1935.

The tour in Malaya was coming to an end. A Memorial Service, attended by 250 all ranks, was held in the Cheras Road Cemetery at K.L. on January 31 for the 24 members of the battalion who had up to then lost their lives in Malaya. The Colonel of the Regiment laid a wreath. General Sir Hugh and Lady Stockwell, the Mentri Besar (Selangor) and numerous other friends were present. After the service, at a parade in K.L., the Deputy Commissioner of Police presented a silver salver to the unit on behalf of the Federation of Malaya Police Force. At Bentong on February 22 The Honourable Teh Eng Suan presented a pair of antique *kris* on behalf of the people of that town.

The Colonel of the Regiment left Malaya by air on February 5 to take up the appointment of General Officer Commanding Berlin (British Sector). The band and drums were at K.L. Airport when he departed. They played "A Hundred Pipers" and "Auld Lang Syne" as he boarded the aircraft.

Pleasant thoughts of the return to England were marred by the death in hospital of Lance-Corporal Newell. He had served in the band of the regiment for 19 years.

At noon on February 24, 1954, the battalion formally handed over its commitments to the 1st Battalion The Royal Hampshire Regiment. That evening The Queen's Own entrained at K.L. for Singapore. The High Commissioner, General Templer, walked through the train to say farewell to the troops and to thank them for the good work they had done.[1]

The emergency in Malaya did not end until July 31, 1960. All officers and other ranks who served in the country between June 18, 1948, and July 31, 1960, received the General Service Medal with the clasp "Malaya". Those of the regiment who had served in Palestine with the 2nd Battalion in 1938-39 received the clasp only, as they already had the medal.

[1]For the story of the 1st Battalion from February 1954 to June 1956 see pages 13-18.

GENERAL SIR GERALD TEMPLER BIDS FAREWELL TO THE 1ST BATTALION, 24TH FEBRUARY, 1954.

A FANFARE ON THE TRUMPETS JUST PRESENTED AT THE BICENTENARY CEREMONY, 31ST OCTOBER, 1956.

THE HELICOPTER IN WHICH THE COLONEL-IN-CHIEF FLEW FROM THE DEPOT SQUARE DURING THE ANNUAL REUNION ON 8TH JULY, 1956.

CHAPTER 3

Culmination

June 1956 — March 1961

1. *Regimental*

JANUARY 7 1956, was the 200*th* anniversary of the raising of The 50th (The Queen's Own) Regiment of Foot. To celebrate it, a programme of special events for the Bicentenary Year was arranged. The main items were to be a presentation of Colours to the 4th/5th Battalion by the Colonel-in-Chief in July; a ceremony of Trooping the Colour by the 1st Battalion at Dover on Sevastopol Day, September 8; and a Bicentenary Ball in London in October. Throughout the year *The Queen's Own Gazette,* in a specially designed cover, contained each month an article on the history and Battle Honours of the regiment.

Two annual events which had an added significance that year were the 18th Regimental Reunion and the Regimental Dinner. The Colonel-in-Chief consented to attend the former at Maidstone on July 8. Her Royal Highness was present at the customary Memorial Service in All Saints' Church, took the salute at the march past in barracks and, after lunching with 300 members of The Past and Present Association, visited the Museum. The Duchess finally left in a helicopter from the Depot square. At the Regimental Dinner at the United Service Club on July 26 the Guest of Honour was the Chief of the Imperial General Staff, General Sir Gerald Templer. The Minister of Defence, Major Sir Walter Monckton, a former

E

officer of the regiment, was present.

The first of the special events, the presentation of Colours to the 4th/5th Battalion, took place as planned. An account of it is in section 4 of this chapter. Trooping the Colour had to be cancelled and the Bicentenary Ball postponed. For at a rally in Alexandria on July 26 Colonel Nasser, the President of Egypt, announced that the Suez Canal had been nationalised.

As the largest user of the Suez Canal, Britain was profoundly affected by this announcement. The canal was an international waterway under an International Convention signed in 1888. Egypt had re-affirmed her determination to uphold this Convention as recently as October 1954. The waterway was owned by the Suez Canal Company, to whom the canal dues, or tolls, were paid. For Britain it was essential that the dues should not be increased and that the canal should remain open for the passage of her ships, particularly of her tankers which brought oil from the Middle East. The British Government therefore announced that it was determined to preserve the canal as an international waterway. The Prime Minister, Sir Anthony Eden, told the House of Commons of "certain precautionary measures of a military nature". These measures included the mobilization and move to Salisbury Plain of the 29th Infantry Brigade, to which the 1st Battalion belonged.

France also made military preparations.

Negotiations concerning the future of the Suez Canal dragged on for three months, first in London, then in Cairo, then in London again, and finally at the Security Council of the United Nations in New York. There, the main part of an Anglo-French resolution was vetoed by Russia. Meanwhile British tankers had been re-routed round the Cape of Good Hope, and petrol had been rationed in the United Kingdom. For the time being a conflict did not seem to be imminent.

The 1st Battalion returned to Dover on September 30. It was then impossible to stage the Trooping the Colour parade before winter set in. A simpler Presentation Ceremony was arranged at Maidstone. A new date was fixed for the Bicentenary Ball.

The Bicentenary Presentation Ceremony took place at the Regimental Depot on the morning of October 31. A large number of spectators, including members of The Past and Present Association,

THE BICENTENARY CEREMONY, 31ST OCTOBER, 1956. THE MAYOR OF GILLINGHAM PRESENTS A TRUMPET TO CPL. MCGOWAN. LIEUT.-GENERAL SIR WILLIAM OLIVER IN CENTRE.

THE BICENTENARY CEREMONY, 31ST OCTOBER, 1956. THE 1ST BATTALION MARCHES PAST THE LORD LIEUTENANT OF KENT.

were there. A cold wind blew across the square as the 1st Battalion marched on parade in No. 1 Dress. Lieutenant-Colonel Buckle was in command. The Colours were brought on by Lieutenant Taylor and 2nd Lieutenant Langhorne. Lord Cornwallis, the Lord Lieutenant of Kent, was received with a general salute. After he had inspected the battalion, the Lord Lieutenant delivered an address. The following presentations were then made to the regiment: eight silver fanfare trumpets with banners by the Boroughs of Maidstone, Rochester, Gravesend, Tunbridge Wells, Chatham, Bromley, Gillingham, Dartford, Beckenham, Bexley and Erith; 14 silver mounted flutes in white cases by the Urban Districts of Chislehurst and Sidcup, Crayford, Northfleet, Orpington, Sevenoaks, Swanscombe and Tonbridge, and the Rural Districts of Dartford, Sevenoaks, Strood and Tonbridge; six embroidered tabards by the Bromley, Chatham, London, Maidstone, 6th Battalion, 7th Battalion and 11th Battalion branches of The Past and Present Association; and two ceremonial Colour belts by The Association of Men of Kent and Kentish Men. A silver bugle was presented to the Regimental Depot by the Rural Districts of Maidstone and Malling. The new Colour belts were received by Lieutenants Heatly and Durtnell,[1] who carried the Colours for the remainder of the parade. As each mayor, chairman or representative made his presentation, he expressed the appreciation of the people of West Kent for the services of The Queen's Own. The Colonel of the Regiment, Lieutenant-General Sir William Oliver, replied. A fanfare was sounded on the new silver trumpets. The 1st Battalion marched past in quick time. The ceremony ended with an advance in review order and a general salute. Afterwards, the past and present officers of the regiment entertained the guests at a luncheon at the Royal Star Hotel, Maidstone.

On that very day a new situation developed in the Middle East. On November 2 the 1st Battalion was at sea bound for Egypt to take part in the Suez Intervention. Despite this, the Bicentenary Ball was not postponed again.

The Bicentenary Ball was held at the Hyde Park Hotel on Friday, November 2. Most of the 1st Battalion officers and their wives were unable to attend, but those of the 4th/5th Battalion and other serving and retired officers with their wives were there in force. Altogether, some 380 people assembled. A display of regimental silver, flanked

[1]Son of Lieutenant-Colonel C. S. Durtnell, O.B.E.

by the Colours of the 1st and 4th/5th Battalions, was in the lobby at the top of the stairs. The Colonel-in-Chief, escorted by her elder son, was met in the lobby by the Colonel of the Regiment and Lady Oliver and the Ball Committee. A bouquet was presented to the Duchess by Mrs. A. R. H. Waring. The Royal party then moved into the Ballroom, where dance music was provided by Mr. T. Kinsman's band. Supper was served at 11.30. The National Anthem was played at 3 a.m.

A Roll of Honour, containing the names of 19,781 officers of the Armies of the Commonwealth who lost their lives on active service between 1939 and 1956, was dedicated at a service in the Chapel of the Royal Military Academy, Sandhurst, on October 23, 1956, in the presence of Queen Elizabeth the Queen Mother. The regiment was represented at the ceremony by Lieutenant-General Sir William Oliver, Major-General Riddell, Lieutenant-Colonel Buckle and Lady Coldstream.[1] The Royal Colonels-in-Chief, including Her Royal Highness The Duchess of Kent, were present. The Book containing the Roll of Honour was dedicated by the Chaplain-General to the Forces, Canon V. J. Pike.

Seven Memorials were unveiled between 1956 and 1961 to those members of the Commonwealth Armies who lost their lives in the Second World War and have no known graves. Near the Memorials are cemeteries in which are buried individuals with named graves. The names of members of the regiment on the Memorials and on the graves were published in the appropriate issues of *The Queen's Own Gazette*. The Memorials were:

Memorial	Campaigns	Date Unveiled	Queen's Own Names	Queen's Own Graves
Groesbeek	From the Seine into Germany, 1944	2. 6.56	1	1
Cassino	Sicily, Italy	30. 9.56	32	123
Dunkirk	N.W. Europe, 1940	29. 6.57	93	2
Medjez-el-Bab	Algeria, Tunisia	18.11.57	54	60

[1]Formerly Mrs. J. H. H. Whitty. See footnote on page 57.

Rangoon	Burma, Assam	9. 2.58	80	70
Brookwood	Britain, Norway, Commando	25.10.58	7	3
Athens	Greece, Crete, Dodecanese, Yugoslavia	10. 5.61	17	9

The Chairman of The Past and Present Association was at the unveiling of the Dunkirk and Brookwood Memorials and laid wreaths on behalf of the regiment.

A five-year plan for the re-organisation of the Armed Forces of Great Britain was announced in July 1957. It provided for an all-volunteer Regular Army of a maximum strength of only 180,000. National Service was to be abolished by the end of 1962. Many soldiers were to be replaced by civilians. New weapons, such as guided missiles with nuclear warheads, were to be issued.

In order to comply with this plan, the Army Council decided that the Infantry of the Line must be reduced from 67 battalions to 52. The cut would be made by the amalgamation of 15 pairs of Regular battalions. One pair would be the 1st Battalion The Buffs (Royal East Kent Regiment) and the 1st Battalion The Queen's Own Royal West Kent Regiment, which would amalgamate, probably in 1961, to form a single regiment of Kent.[1] The Regular battalions in each brigade would wear a brigade cap badge. The Territorial battalions would retain their cap badges and their titles. Regimental Depots would close, and recruits would be trained at Brigade Depots.

The amalgamation with The Buffs presented numerous problems, and a Queen's Own Amalgamation Committee was set up to deal with them. This committee consisted of Lieutenant-Colonel Edwards (Chairman), a retired officer, representatives from the Regimental Depot and the 1st and 4th/5th Battalions, and a secretary (Lieutenant-

[1]There was another amalgamation in the Home Counties Brigade: the 1st Battalion The Queen's Royal Regiment (West Surrey) with the 1st Battalion The East Surrey Regiment to form The Queen's Royal Surrey Regiment.

Colonel Eason). The Buffs set up a similar committee. Later on, the two committees met on a number of occasions, alternately at Maidstone and Canterbury, as a Joint Amalgamation Committee. Its decisions and all other matters concerning the amalgamation are dealt with in chapter 5.

The officers were honoured by the presence of the Colonel-in-Chief at the Regimental Dinner at the United Service Club on May 9, 1958. Before and after the dinner a number of officers were presented to Her Royal Highness. The guests included the Lord Lieutenant of Kent, the Deputy Colonel of The Buffs and the officer commanding The Buffs' Depot. That year the Colonel of The Queen's Own and the officer commanding The Queen's Own Depot were guests at The Buffs' Regimental Dinner.

The British Automatic Rifle (Self-loading Rifle 7.62 mm L.I.A.I.), with a magazine holding 20 rounds, gradually replaced the Lee-Enfield in the British Army. It was issued to the 1st Battalion in Cyprus early in 1957. One hundred were received by the Regimental Depot in December 1958, and 110 more in January 1960. The 4th/5th Battalion received 50 at the end of 1960. Owing to the shape of the new rifle, some changes had to be made in the arms drill. The main difference was that sloping arms was abolished.

The Golden Jubilee of the Territorial Army was celebrated in 1958. In connection with it, a detachment of the 4th/5th Battalion took part in a Royal Review of the Territorial Army in Hyde Park on June 21. The 4th/5th played a more prominent role in the celebrations at Maidstone on July 5 and at Canterbury on July 6. (See section 4 of this chapter.)

Lieutenant-Colonel K. S. Kersey and five other members of The Essex and Kent Scottish, who had come from Canada on duty, visited Maidstone on November 10, 1958. In the morning they were entertained by the Mayor in his Parlour. After lunch in the Depot officers' mess, they went round the Regimental Museum and took part in a shooting match on the miniature range. In the evening they were guests at a dinner in the Depot officers' mess. Five Nigerian officer cadets, who were attached to the Depot at the time, were also at the dinner. This Commonwealth occasion ended with the presentation by the Colonel of the Regiment to The Essex and Kent Scottish of an original water-colour depicting sentries of The 97th Foot at Halifax, Nova Scotia, in about 1878.

MAJOR-GENERAL D. E. B. TALBOT, C.B., C.B.E., D.S.O., M.C., COLONEL OF THE QUEEN'S OWN FROM OCTOBER, 1959, TO MARCH, 1961.

Because of a printers' strike, *The Queen's Own Gazette* was not published in July 1959. A duplicated news-sheet was sent out instead. This was the first occasion since March 1888 that the regimental journal had not appeared. (See Appendix G for a brief history of *The Queen's Own Gazette.*)

The regiment was represented by Major Weymouth at a ceremony held on July 30, 1959, at Corunna to commemorate the 150th anniversary of the Battle of Corunna and the death of Sir John Moore. In that battle, which was fought on January 16, 1809, The 50th (West Kent) Regiment played a prominent part.

The cap badge of the Home Counties Brigade, a Saxon crown with an upward pointing sword, was adopted by the infantry regiments of the counties of Kent, Middlesex. Surrey and Sussex on October 14, 1959.[1] From that date all ranks of The Queen's Own, except the 4th/5th Battalion and any Regulars serving with it, ceased to wear the regimental cap badge.

Lieutenant-General Sir William Oliver, who had been Principal Staff Officer to the Minister for Commonwealth Relations for the previous two years, left England in October 1959 to take up the appointment of High Commissioner to the United Kingdom in Australia. At a farewell cocktail party in the Depot officers' mess on October 15, he was presented with a pair of inscribed candelabra as a token of appreciation of his outstanding work for the regiment over 11 momentous years. He was succeeded as Colonel of the Regiment by Major-General D. E. B. Talbot, C.B.E., D.S.O., M.C.

Since his return from New Zealand in 1951, General Talbot had been on the Staff at the War Office, had commanded two different brigades in Malaya, and had been B.G.S. (Staff Duties) at the headquarters of the British Army of the Rhine. At the time of his appointment as Colonel of the Regiment, he was General Officer Commanding East Anglian District and 54th (East Anglian) Division, with headquarters at Colchester. He was made a C.B. in the New Year Honours List in January 1960.

The Canterbury Regiment of New Zealand celebrated its centenary in 1959. To mark the occasion, a silver bugle was presented to this allied regiment by all ranks of The Queen's Own.

As the Regimental Depot was due to close early in 1961, it was

[1]The Royal Fusiliers went into the Fusilier Brigade.

necessary to establish the Regimental Museum elsewhere. The Maidstone Museum Committee solved this problem by offering a room in the Maidstone Museum. The contents of the Regimental Museum were transferred from the barracks to this room in the spring of 1960. The room, known as The Queen's Own Room in the Maidstone Museum, was opened by Mrs. Talbot on June 9. Major Love continued as curator.

Before the contents of the Regimental Museum were moved from the barracks, some exhibits were sent "on long loan" elsewhere. Among the items were:

To the National Army Museum at Sandhurst—One of the Sutlej guns; a shako of the Kent Rifle Volunteers; breast-plates of The 50th, The 97th and the West Kent Militia; salad plates of The 50th; four volumes of the Regimental History.

To the Home Counties Brigade Museum at Canterbury—Five pictures, including the Battle of Neuve Chapelle; four tunics, including a shell-jacket of The 97th; three head-dresses; 28 weapons of various kinds; items of German equipment of the 1914-18 and the 1939-45 Wars; two helmet plates; a set of medals; four volumes of the Regimental History.

Three photostat copies were made of the Historical Records of the regiment, 1756-1939. One copy was sent to the War Office Library, one to the Library of the Royal United Service Institution, and the third was kept at Regimental Headquarters. The original records, written in longhand, were placed in The Queen's Own Room in the Maidstone Museum.

A re-organisation of the Territorial Army was announced in November 1960. The 4th/5th Battalion was not affected. But the 265th Light Anti-Aircraft Regiment (T.A.) was amalgamated with two other units to form a new Light Anti-Aircraft Regiment (T.A.) centred on Napier Barracks, Baring Road, Grove Park, London, S.E.12. Q (The Queen's Own) Battery, the sub-unit of the 265th L.A.A. Regiment which was affiliated to The Queen's Own, disappeared. Most of its members went into the Headquarter Troop of a battery at Napier Barracks. Affiliation to The Queen's Own ceased. Holly Hedge House, Blackheath, was taken over by a Parachute Regiment (T.A.).

That year (1960), the last before the amalgamation with The Buffs, the Colonel-in-Chief honoured the regiment with her presence at both the Regimental Dinner and the Annual Reunion. The Duchess also visited the 1st Battalion at Shorncliffe and the 4th/5th in camp at Dibgate nearby. At the dinner, which was held at the United Service Club on May 13, Her Royal Highness proposed the toast of The Queen's Own. She said:

"I cannot let this occasion pass without saying a very few words to you all. I must, of course, be rather careful because I have the Colonel of The Buffs sitting on my right. But he will certainly agree that this is a very special occasion in the history of our regiment. I have thought of you all so much during the past few months, and I am so glad that I can share this evening with you. Of one thing I am completely sure: despite all the changes that are to come about, I can depend upon you all to make them go smoothly, and I am confident that the regiment, in its new form, will be a very happy and fine one indeed. Gentlemen, I ask you now to join me in drinking—for the last time—the toast of The Queen's Own."

Lieutenant-General Sir James O'Dowda, K.C.B., C.S.I., C.M.G, who had been Colonel of the Regiment from December 1927 until September 1936, died at Rye on January 2, 1961.

At its final meeting on February 27, 1961, the Regimental Council decided to set up a Museum Committee to administer the Regimental Museum, which was housed in The Queen's Own Room in the Maidstone Museum. The original composition of this committee was:

Chairman: Major-General D. E. B. Talbot.

Vice-Chairman: Brigadier A. R. Fyler.

Members: The Honorary Colonel of the 4th/5th Battalion (ex officio).

The Commanding Officer of the 4th/5th Battalion (ex officio).

Lieutenant-Colonel H. N. Edwards.

Lieutenant-Colonel H. D. Chaplin.

Lieutenant-Colonel D. H. Gwilliam.

Lieutentant-General Sir William Oliver.

Lieutenant-Colonel H. O. Lovell.

Lieutenant-Colonel H. W. Styles.
Major de S. H. Lewis-Barned.
Captain P. F. Haynes.
Mr. H. W. Maxlow.

Co-opted: The Curator of the Regimental Museum.
The Curator of the Maidstone Museum.

Secretary: Lieutenant-Colonel A. A. Eason.

The Chairman, Vice-Chairman and the first five members were Managing Trustees responsible for the Regimental Museum Fund.

Subsequently, Colonel Eason was replaced as secretary by Lieutenant-Colonel M. R. L. Grove, but became a member of the Committee; Lieutenant-Colonels G. E. L. Pardington and H. B. H. Waring joined the Committee as additional members.

Besides the administration of the museum, the Museum Committee was empowered to deal with any regimental matters which might arise after March 1 1961, the date fixed for the amalgamation.

The Museum Committee set up a sub-committee, under Colonel R. O. Pulverman, to investigate the implications, particularly financial, of a Regimental Chapel being established within All Saints' Church, Maidstone. Into this chapel could be moved some of the regimental memorials which are in other parts of the church. The Haifa Lectern[1] and the Malayan Memorial Tablet[2] could be placed in it.

★ ★ ★

The following members of The Queen's Own won Army Championships or represented the Army or a County at sport:

1958. Lieutenant Heatly (attached to The Parachute Regiment) played hockey for the Army on several occasions.

1959. Lance-Corporal O'Connell (Depot) boxed for the Army against the Royal Air Force and the Royal Netherlands Army.

1959. Lieutenant Heatly (attached to The Parachute Regiment) played hockey for the Army against the R.M.A., Sandhurst.

[1]See page 6. [2]See page 44.

1960. Private Cocozza (1st Battalion) played association football for Sussex.

1960. Lieutenant Heatly (attached to The Parachute Regiment) played hockey for the Army against the Royal Navy and the Royal Air Force.

1960. Corporal O'Connell (Depot) won the Army and the Imperial Services Light Welterweight Boxing Championships and boxed for the Army against Poland.

1960. Lieutenant Whitty[1] (Depot) played cricket for the Army against the Civil Service and the Club Cricket Conference.

1960. Private Kirby (1st Battalion) won the 4,000 metres pursuit race in the Army Cycling Championships.

2. *The Regimental Depot*

The last six months of 1956, the Bicentenary Year, was a notable period at the Regimental Depot. On July 20 two squads of recruits and all available members of the Permanent Staff and their families went to Tonbridge for the Presentation of Colours to the 4th/5th Battalion. On September 9, the day after the Sevastopol celebrations and dance, the Depot provided one of the guards at the laying-up of the Colours of the 4th and 5th Battalions in All Saints' Church. For a week before this, there were five stands of Colours in the barracks. These were the Colours of the 1st Battalion, which had been mobilized; those of the 2nd Battalion, which had been amalgamated with the 1st; those of the 3rd, which had been disbanded; and those of the 4th and 5th Battalions, which had been amalgamated to form the 4th/5th.[2] On October 31, all the Depot staff and recruits watched the Bicentenary Presentation Ceremony on the square; they had previously made all the administrative arrangements for it.

When the 1st Battalion hastily left Dover on November 2 to take part in the Suez Intervention, its rear party and the band were

[1]Son of Lieutenant-Colonel J. H. H. Whitty, D.S.O., M.C., of The Queen's Own, who was killed in Italy in October 1944.

[2]The Colours of the 3rd Battalion were in the Museum; the others were in the officers' mess for safe-keeping. The Colours of the 2nd Battalion were placed in the Museum in June 1961.

attached to the Regimental Depot. Major Sivers, the Quartermaster, and others of the Permanent Staff went to Dover to assist in returning stores and handing over barracks. Captain Stephens, then Quartermaster of the 4th/5th, came over from Tonbridge to help with the additional work. Two weeks later, the 1st Battalion rear party moved to the Depot; the band remained at Dover a little longer.

On New Year's Eve, at about 11 p.m., 285 Reservists arrived from the 1st Battalion in Cyprus. Major Sivers had a meal ready for them and arranged accommodation for all of them in the barracks for the night. Next morning the gymnasium became a release centre, in which the 285 men were medically inspected by three doctors, paid and documented. Before lunch-time most of them had departed to their homes. The remainder were cleared during the afternoon.

The 1st Battalion band was at Orpington on June 15, 1957, when The Duchess of Kent laid the foundation stone of the new parish church. It sounded a fanfare on the Bicentenary silver trumpets as Her Royal Highness arrived, and accompanied the hymns during the service. Afterwards, it marched through Orpington.

During September the band played in Rochester Cathedral on Battle of Britain Sunday, and, together with the bands of the Royal Marines, the Royal Engineers and The Buffs, performed at a United Services Tattoo at Gillingham. It embarked in the troopship "Dilwara" on October 31 to join the 1st Battalion in Cyprus.

An intake of 60 National Servicemen arrived in November to be trained for The Royal Fusiliers. Two intakes, both of 90 men, arrived in January and February 1958. These large intakes were part of the plan to abolish National Service. Another sign of the times was that the draft which left for the 1st Battalion in August 1958 went by air instead of by troopship.

The outstanding boxer in the regiment at that time was Corporal O'Connell. Before he enlisted, he was a member of the Royal Ordnance Factory Boxing Club at Erith. He began his National Service in November 1958 and was retained at the Regimental Depot as a Physical Training Instructor. Having boxed for the Army twice in 1959, he won the Army Light Welterweight Championship at Aldershot in March 1960 and went on to win the Imperial Services Championship at Portsmouth in April. He had a trial for the Olympic Games in May. In January 1961, a few weeks after his release from

National Service, O'Connell boxed for England against Scotland and West Germany.

The passing-out parades at the Depot were memorable occasions. They were attended by many relatives and friends of the recruits. Among the officers who inspected the parades were the Colonel of the Regiment, the G.O.C. Home Counties District, and the Brigade Colonel. After each parade, a religious service was held in the drill shed. It was followed by a Physical Training Display, a demonstration on the assault course, and tea in the gymnasium.

As other Regimental Depots closed or became full of recruits, so more intakes for different regiments were trained by The Queen's Own. In 1960 there were 88 men for the East Anglian Brigade, 74 for The Buffs, 62 for The Queen's Royal Surrey Regiment, 47 for The Royal Sussex Regiment and 34 for The Middlesex Regiment under training at Maidstone at various times, besides well over 100 for The Queen's Own. The last intake of National Servicemen arrived at the Regimental Depot in August. The final call-up in Britain was on November 17. After that, a squad of 25 Regular recruits for The Queen's Own was formed at Maidstone. It was passed out by the Colonel of the Regiment on February 10, 1961.

The farewell parade of the Regimental Depot took place on February 28, 1961, in the presence of His Worship the Mayor of Maidstone and members of the Corporation. The parade was inspected by the Mayor, who also delivered an address. The Colonel of the Regiment replied. Before the troops marched off, a presentation of two wine jugs was made to the Mayor and Corporation by General Talbot to commemorate the close and happy association between the regiment and the Borough of Maidstone throughout 87 years.

On March 1 the Regimental Depot became the Depot of The Queen's Own Buffs, The Royal Kent Regiment. It closed on March 31. From that date all recruits for The Queen's Own Buffs were trained at the Home Counties Brigade Depot at Canterbury. A maintenance party remained in the barracks at Maidstone until June 30, when they were handed over to the Officer in Charge of Barracks.

3. *The 1st Battalion at Dover, Bulford and Shorncliffe*

The 1st Battalion arrived at Dover Priory Station on June 9, 1956, and went into Old Park Barracks. These barracks, which are to the east of the town, were the most modern in Dover. Nevertheless, as they had been occupied recently only by units in transit, they were in a poor condition and required much cleaning and some repair.

After seven days' disembarkation leave, the battalion made preparations for Trooping the Colour as part of the Regimental Bicentenary celebrations. Company training started. The annual classification courses were fired on the ranges nearby.

A Guard of Honour of three officers and 100 other ranks was mounted at Dover Marine Station on July 16 for King Feisal of Iraq, who was making a State visit to Britain. Captain Fletcher was in command, Lieutenant Heatly was subaltern of the guard, Lieutenant Neve carried the Queen's Colour. The guard wore No. 1 Dress with white equipment.

The Chief of the Imperial General Staff, General Sir Gerald Templer, visited the battalion on July 25.

After Colonel Nasser had announced on July 26 that the Suez Canal had been nationalised, the battalion, less one company, went to Dibgate, near Shorncliffe, and took over the administration of three cadet camps from an anti-aircraft unit, which had been ordered to mobilize. The cadets, over 2,000 of them, completed their training and departed. By August 8 the whole battalion was back at Dover.

Meanwhile the 3rd Infantry Division (Major-General J. B. Churcher), to which the 1st Battalion belonged, had received orders to mobilize. Between August 4 and 11 about 350 Reservists arrived at Old Park Barracks to bring the battalion up to war establishment. Some of them were Queen's Own; the rest were from every regiment in the Home Counties and East Anglian Brigades. That part of the mobilization procedure went well. But the mobilization stores and equipment had to be collected in motor transport from various places. It was 14 days before everything had been obtained. The Colours were taken to the Regimental Depot. The silver was placed in a bank at Maidstone. Khaki drill uniform was issued.

It seemed probable that the 3rd Infantry Division would move at short notice to a concentration area in the Near East. Orders were issued for the despatch of some of the vehicles of the battalion to Malta.

Most of the vehicles of the 1st Battalion, loaded with weapons and stores, were driven to the ports of embarkation in two groups. The first, under Captain Osborne, left Dover on August 21. The second, under Sergeant Brown (the M.T. Sergeant), went a few days later. The first group reached Plymouth on the 22nd and, after a wait of two days, some of the vehicles were loaded in the L.S.T. " Suvla," which arrived in Malta on September 1. The other vehicles in this group could not be loaded at Plymouth and did not arrive in Malta until October 3. Sergeant Brown's group arrived on the island on September 10. In Malta the Vehicle Party was at first accommodated in Fort St. Elmo in Valetta. It moved on October 10 to a tented camp in the grounds of the United Services Sports Club at Marsa. The Marsa Club was the place where the headquarters of the 2nd Battalion had been for two years during the 1939-1945 War.

The 29th Infantry Brigade, consisting of the 1st Battalion The Royal Fusiliers, the 1st Battalion The York and Lancaster Regiment and the 1st Battalion The Queen's Own, moved by rail from Dover to Salisbury Plain on August 24. The whole brigade went under canvas at Bulford Fields. As soon as the personnel had settled in, intensive training for war began.

Towards the end of August, Lieutenant-Colonel Buckle, the commanding officer of the 1st Battalion, was called to the War Office to be briefed. A provisional plan for military action against Egypt was explained to him. As the weeks went by, details of the plan were frequently changed. The type of transport to be used varied almost from day to day. At times it was a troopship, at others an aircraft carrier or aircraft. Once, C Company was under orders to join the Vehicle Party in Malta. One part of the plan which was not altered was that The Queen's Own would be the first infantry to land.

Although most of its vehicles and its support weapons, except the Vickers machine guns, were on the way to Malta, the 1st Battalion got down to training in earnest. Night operations, and desert warfare and street fighting exercises were carried out. A vast amount of ammunition was expended on the ranges. Before long, all ranks were battle-fit. The things that were most remembered by those that were there were the heavy rain, wet clothes, the mud, the many rumours of departure, and the frequent change of orders. Although the Reservists found it hard to understand why they were kept waiting, their morale remained high.

On September 23 the British and French Governments requested the President of the Security Council of the United Nations to call a meeting of the Council to consider the situation created by the Egyptian Government in nationalising the Suez Canal. As the discussion in the Security Council was likely to continue for some time, the 29th Infantry Brigade was ordered to return to barracks.

The 1st Battalion moved back to Dover in two special trains on September 30. Stores were unpacked. The Colours and the silver were obtained from Maidstone. The Reservists were sent on short leave. Thoughts of war were put aside. Drill parades were held in preparation for the Bicentenary Presentation Ceremony, which was to take place on October 31.

Events then took a dramatic turn. Israel invaded Egypt on October 29.

Most of the battalion went by road to the Regimental Depot on October 30 and carried out a rehearsal of the Bicentenary parade. The troops were accommodated in the barracks at Maidstone for the night.

On the afternoon of the 30th the British and French Governments sent an ultimatum to Israel and Egypt to stop all warlike action. If one or both had not undertaken to comply within 12 hours, British and French forces would intervene so as to bring hostilities to an end.

On the evening of the 30th the Colonel of the Regiment, then Vice-Chief of the Imperial General Staff, told the officers of the 1st Battalion that if the ultimatum was not accepted the battalion would probably embark for Egypt on November 2. General Oliver also said that he would leave it to them to decide whether the Bicentenary Presentation Ceremony should be cancelled. It was decided that the ceremony must take place, but that some key officers and the colour-sergeants would return to Dover forthwith.

During the night Israel accepted the ultimatum. Egypt rejected it.

As already recorded, the Bicentenary Presentation Ceremony took place at the Regimental Depot on the morning of October 31. The 1st Battalion returned to Dover in the afternoon and began to pack. The Colours were left at the Depot. The silver was crated again and sent to Maidstone.

On the morning of November 2 the battalion went by train to Southampton, where the personnel embarked in the "Asturias" for

Egypt. The Vickers guns and the remaining vehicles, under Captain Mansfield, were loaded in the L.S.T. " Cymric." This was a much slower ship. It took a week longer than the "Asturias " to complete the voyage.

The battalion was overseas for nearly three years, first in Egypt and then in Cyprus. For most of that time it was on active service. The story is told in the next chapter.

★ ★ ★

The advanced party of the 1st Battalion, under Major Elgood (the 2nd-in-command), arrived at Southampton from Cyprus in the troopship " Dilwara " on August 8, 1959. Most of the men went on leave from the ship. The others travelled by train to Shorncliffe. The take-over of Moore Barracks and the married quarters was completed by September 8.

The main body came home from Cyprus in the " Devonshire." The troopship entered the Grand Harbour, Malta, on October 3. Shore leave was granted. While many of the men explored Valetta, Lieutenant-Colonel Gwilliam (the commanding officer) took a small party ashore to lay two wreaths in memory of those of the 2nd Battalion who lost their lives during the siege of the island in 1940-1942. R.Q.M.S. Simpson and Colour-Sergeant Vine, who had both been there during the siege, laid the wreaths. Simpson placed one at the foot of the War Memorial in Floriana; Vine laid the other over The Queen's Own graves in Imtarfa Military Cemetery.

Colonel Gwilliam gave permission for 12 rank and file to disembark at Malta and make their own way home across Europe.

After the " Devonshire " had drawn alongside the quay at Southampton the B.B.C., the Press and a number of distinguished visitors were soon on board. The visitors included Lieutenant-General Sir William Oliver; Major-General Talbot; Brigadier Jackson, who was commanding the brigade into which the battalion was going; and Lieutenant-Colonels Buckle and Flint. Among the many messages of welcome were telegrams from the Colonel-in-Chief, the Chief of the Imperial General Staff, the Mayor of Maidstone, and the London and Bromley branches of The Past and Present Association. General Oliver addressed the battalion and bade farewell as Colonel of the Regiment.

Disembarkation was carried out efficiently on October 11. All ranks went straight on leave.

When the whole battalion had assembled in Moore Barracks from leave early in December, training began for the role of strategic reserve as part of the 19th Infantry Brigade Group. Individual fitness tests, route marches of increasing length, and cadre courses for N.C.O.s in stamina and leadership were carried out. This period ended in February 1960 with an inter-platoon night raiding contest. For this the troops wore combat dress and the new pattern web equipment, which had recently been received.

Earlier in February all available officers, about 20 senior N.C.O.s and some members of the M.T. Platoon attended a short course in Air Portability at the Army Air Transport Training and Development Centre at Old Sarum. During the course they were introduced by Colonel Crook and his staff to the intricacies of planning an air move and the methods of loading aircraft.

At the beginning of March the battalion, equipped as for war, drove out of barracks in fully-loaded vehicles and carried out a simulated air movement at Crowborough. This was followed by an amphibious exercise, which began at Poole Harbour and ended at Lulworth Cove. On March 21 the battalion became the stand-by unit for all strategic reserve commitments. This meant that two companies had to be at immediate readiness.

The tour of duty in the Strategic Reserve ended on June 1. From that date the battalion came under the direct command of Headquarters Home Counties District.

The civic honour of adoption was conferred upon the battalion by the Borough of Folkestone on May 16. The ceremony took place on The Leas. Some 300 all ranks, including the band and drums, were on parade. The Queen's Colour was carried by Lieutenant Champion, the Regimental by 2nd Lieutenant Schooling. The Town Clerk read the resolution of adoption, which was encased in a leather container. The Mayor, Alderman W. Harris, presented it to the commanding officer and addressed the parade. Colonel Gwilliam replied. The battalion then marched past, the salute being taken by the Mayor, who was accompanied by the Colonel of the Regiment. Afterwards, the senior officers were entertained by the Town Council at a reception in the Leas Cliff Hall.

THE 1909-1956 QUEEN'S COLOUR OF THE 4TH BATTALION.

THE 1909-1956 REGIMENTAL COLOUR OF THE 4TH BATTALION.
THESE TWO COLOURS WERE LAID UP ON 9TH SEPTEMBER, 1956.

THE 1909-1947 KING'S COLOUR OF THE 5TH BATTALION.

THE 1909-1947 REGIMENTAL COLOUR OF THE 5TH BATTALION.
THESE TWO COLOURS WERE LAID UP ON 9TH SEPTEMBER, 1956.

The Regimental Colour was trooped before the Colonel-in-Chief on Sir John Moore Plain, Shorncliffe, on June 10. The Duchess was met by Major-General Talbot. Captain Cleaver acted as A.D.C. to Her Royal Highness. Colonel Gwilliam commanded the parade. The Colour was carried by 2nd Lieutenant Schooling. Lieutenant Champion was in command of the escort. The R.S.M. was W.O.I Parker. The four guard commanders were Captain Leigh, Major Osborne, Captain West (The Buffs) and Captain Mannering. After the Colour had been trooped, the four guards marched past in slow and quick time to " The Men of Kent " and "A Hundred Pipers." Over 2,000 spectators, including many members of The Past and Present Association, were there.

After the ceremony, the Duchess attended a reception in a marquee, where a number of guests were presented to her. Among them were the Mayors of Folkestone and Boulogne and several boroughs in West Kent. Her Royal Highness then visited the sergeants in their mess and lunched in the officers' mess. She finally left in an open Land Rover to visit the 4th/5th Battalion in camp at Dibgate.

In the last week of June, some of the personnel went to Eastbourne to take part in a Military Tattoo organised by Colonel Grace, the Brigade Colonel. D Company performed the bulk of the administrative duties. The Support Company gave a spectacular demonstration of an infantry raid. The band and drums, together with the bands and drums of The Queen's Royal Surrey Regiment and The Buffs, gave a Massed Bands Display under the direction of Bandmaster Watkins and Drum-Major Clark. The Tattoo was repeated on the night of June 29 at Folkestone Police Sports.

Most of the battalion went to North Wales for four weeks in the summer to administer a cadet camp in Kinmel Park. All ranks then departed on a month's leave. September was spent in camp at Wretham in Norfolk. The camp was near the Stanford Practical Training Area, on which field firing, battalion schemes, and a ten days' exercise against the 19th Infantry Brigade were carried out.

As the date for the amalgamation with The Buffs drew near, the battalion gradually diminished in numbers. D Company was disbanded.

The 1st Battalion The Buffs, under the command of Lieutenant-Colonel Dendy, disembarked at Folkestone from Germany on November 21. They were played ashore by the band of The Queen's

Own. Lieutenant-Colonel Gwilliam, R.S.M. Parker and Drum-Major Clark met them on the quay. They went in buses to Ross Barracks, which are next to Moore Barracks at Shorncliffe.

The amalgamation of the two battalions began after the Christmas holiday. Some Buffs moved from Ross to Moore Barracks, some of The Queen's Own moved from Moore to Ross Barracks. On January 10, 1961, the companies mustered as follows:—

In Moore Barracks

H.Q. Company (H.Q. Companies of both units)

A Company (A Companies of both units)

B Company (B Company of The Buffs and C of The Queen's Own).

In Ross Barracks

C Company (C Company of The Buffs and elements of both H.Q. Companies)

D Company (D Company of The Buffs and B of The Queen's Own)

Support Company (the Support Companies of both units).

The officers' and sergeants' messes were merged in the middle of February.

Orders were issued in the names of both commanding officers until March 1. On that day all companies came under the command of Lieutenant-Colonel Dendy, as the first commanding officer of the 1st Battalion The Queen's Own Buffs, The Royal Kent Regiment.

The last Regular officer to be commissioned into The Queen's Own was 2nd Lieutenant B. K. Donovan. The final Order of Battle of the 1st Battalion The Queen's Own is in Appendix E.

4. *The 4th/5th Battalion (T.A.)*

For the 4th/5th Battalion the most memorable event of the Regimental Bicentenary Year was the presentation of Colours by the Colonel-in-Chief. This took place on the Angel Ground at Tonbridge on the afternoon of Friday, July 20, 1956. Several rehearsals of the

THE COLOURS PRESENTED TO THE 4TH/5TH BATTALION ON 20TH JULY, 1956.

THE 4TH/5TH BATTALION MARCHING PAST THE COLONEL-IN-CHIEF AFTER THE PRESENTATION OF COLOURS, 20TH JULY, 1956.

ceremony had been held at camp on St. Martin's Plain, Shorncliffe, during the previous week. The Colours were consecrated by Canon V. J. Pike, Chaplain-General to the Forces. Lieutenant Nyren received the Queen's Colour, and Lieutenant Rainbow the Regimental. The R.S.M. was W.O.1 Watts. After Her Royal Highness had presented the Colours, she addressed the battalion. Lieutenant-Colonel Keenlyside,[1] the commanding officer, replied. The troops then marched past and advanced in review order. The music was played by the band of the 1st Battalion. After the ceremony the Duchess drove to Tonbridge Castle, where she took tea with the officers on the lawn. Captain Robson acted as A.D.C. to Her Royal Highness throughout the day.

The Old Colours of the 4th and 5th Battalions were laid up in All Saints' Church, Maidstone, on Sunday September 9. They were carried from the Regimental Depot to the church by Lieutenants Nyren and Maclachlan (4th) and Lieutenants Watson and Pedgrift (5th). The escort consisted of two guards. No. 1, which was provided by the 4th/5th Battalion, was commanded by Major Coath. No. 2, under Major H. B. H. Waring,[2] was found by the Depot Permanent Staff and recruits. The band of the 1st Battalion played during the service. After the last hymn, the Colonel of the Regiment requested the Rev. K. Watts, the curate, to receive the Colours into his hands for safe-keeping. The Colours were borne by Lieutenant-Colonel Keenlyside and Major A. R. H. Waring[2] to the altar rails, where the curate took them and laid them on the altar. The ceremony ended with the National Anthem.

Annual training for 1957 was from May 4-18 at Castlemartin in Pembrokeshire. The whole of the 133rd Brigade was in the camp which, except for the cookhouses and ablution rooms, was under canvas. There was a splendid bathing beach some five miles away for those hardy enough to swim at that time of the year. In the camp a cinema run by the Army Kinema Corporation gave two programmes each evening. The training areas, which were nearby, were fully used for minor tactical exercises such as night patrolling.

[1]Son of Captain G. F. H. Keenlyside, of The Queen's Own, who died of wounds received at Neuve Chapelle in October 1914.

[2]Sons of Lieutenant-Colonel H. A. Waring, D.S.O., who was adjutant of the 3rd Battalion (Reserve) from 1912 to 1915 and of the 1st Battalion from 1916 to 1917.

The support weapons were fired on a battle training ground, which was also close at hand. The band of the 1st Battalion came from the Depot for the first week and played at a dance for all ranks, at a concert in the N.A.A.F.I. canteen, and at guest nights in the officers' messes. Its last engagement was a Brigade Church Parade.

After this parade Major A. R. H. Waring assumed command. He was the first Territorial officer to command the battalion since Lieutenant-Colonel Defrates had relinquished the appointment in June 1948.

The drill hall in Bank Street, Tonbridge, was vacated in October 1957, when those elements of the unit which had been using it moved into the T.A. Centre in Avebury Avenue. This centre had recently been enlarged, with a new garage at one end and additional accommodation at the other. The upper floor had also been extended. The new premises were officially opened by Lord Cornwallis, the Lord Lieutenant of Kent, on October 12. After the ceremony, the battalion was At Home to some 300 guests.

In 1958 the annual camp was at Barry, some ten miles from Dundee in Scotland. The advanced party made the long journey by road in the vehicles of the battalion; the main body went by rail. The training programme included a rifle meeting, the firing of the support weapons, and a battalion and a brigade exercise.

The Jubilee (the 50th Anniversary) of the Territorial Army was celebrated in 1958. The national celebration was a Royal Review, which took place in Hyde Park on Sunday June 22. Her Majesty Queen Elizabeth II inspected the parade and took the salute at the march past. The 4th/5th Battalion was represented by four officers and 14 other ranks. Major Meyrick commanded the contingent. Captain Watson was his 2nd-in-command. Lieutenant Morley-Jacob carried the Queen's Colour and Lieutenant Maclachlan the Regimental.

The regimental celebration was at Maidstone on Saturday July 5. The 4th/5th, a detachment of cadets and the band of the 3rd Battalion The Parachute Regiment marched from the Depot to the Regimental Cenotaph in Brenchley Gardens, where a drumhead service was held. The Colours were carried by Lieutenants Morley-Jacob and Nyren. The Mayors of Maidstone, Tunbridge Wells, Bromley and Beckenham, and the Chairmen of the Urban District Councils of Tonbridge, Orpington, Sevenoaks, Penge and Southborough attended the service.

THE DRUMHEAD SERVICE IN BRENCHLEY GARDENS DURING THE T.A. JUBILEE CELEBRATIONS, 5TH JULY, 1958.

THE 4TH/5TH BATTALION MARCHING PAST THE COLONEL-IN-CHIEF AT CANTERBURY, 6TH JULY, 1958.

The whole parade then marched back to the barracks. There, the Colonel of the Regiment took the salute at a march past, after which tea was served on the back field. The proceedings ended with the drums of the 1st Cadet Battalion beating retreat. Later, the guests were entertained at a dinner in the drill shed and a band concert in the gymnasium.

The T.A. Jubilee was celebrated by the county of Kent at Canterbury on Sunday July 6. The 4th/5th, together with the two Territorial battalions of The Buffs, paraded at Wemyss Barracks and marched to the Cathedral for a special service. Her Royal Highness The Duchess of Kent, the Lord Lieutenant and other officials of the county were present. After the service, the parade re-formed in the precincts of the Cathedral. The Duchess took the salute in Broad Street. Captain Calver-Jones acted as her A.D.C. for the day. The Colours of the 4th/5th were again carried by Lieutenants Morley-Jacob and Nyren.

The final event in connection with the T.A. Jubilee took place on November 7. It was a reception for C Company of the 4th/5th given by the Sevenoaks Urban District Council in the Council Chambers. The drums of the battalion were piled in the foyer. The Colours and the silver were displayed.

1959 was the centennial year of the battalion. For there was unbroken historical continuity between the Tonbridge Rifle Volunteer Corps, which was formed in 1859, and the 4th/5th. To mark the occasion, a short account of the 100 years of voluntary service of the battalion was published in *The Queen's Own Gazette* in January and February 1959.

Annual training in 1959 was carried out at the Army School of Civil Defence at Epsom from June 21 to July 4. For the fortnight the battalion was accommodated in huts and "spiders" at Pendell Camp, Mersham, between Godstone and Redhill. The object was to train all ranks in advanced rescue duties in aid of the Civil Defence Services. Not only was it an instructive and enjoyable course, but it also provided a welcome change from the customary tactical training.

By 1960 the Permanent Staff was considerably larger than it had been in 1951. The Regular Army staff consisted of a Training Major, who was also the Adjutant, a Quartermaster, an R.S.M., six instructors (one for each company), an M.T. corporal and a driver. The civilian staff comprised a Chief Clerk and three assistants, two storemen (one for the Quartermaster and one for the M.T. Platoon), two storemen-clerks, two drivers, and six caretakers (one for each drill hall). There were no fewer than 30 vehicles on charge—seven jeeps (Champs and Land Rovers), 13 trucks, two half-track vehicles and eight motor cycles.

The Colonel-in-Chief honoured the battalion by a visit on June 10, 1960, while it was in camp at Dibgate. Her Royal Highness, who was accompanied by the Colonel of the Regiment, arrived at about 3 p.m. from Shorncliffe, where she had seen the 1st Battalion troop the Colour. At the entrance to camp she was met by Lieutenant-Colonel A. R. H. Waring and inspected a Guard of Honour commanded by Major Innes; the Queen's Colour was carried by Lieutenant Finnis. The Duchess then watched a series of training demonstrations. She visited the sergeants' mess and took tea with the officers and their wives before leaving for Lympne Airport on her journey back to London.

When The Queen's Own Buffs, The Royal Kent Regiment was formed in March 1961, the 4th/5th Battalion took its place as one of the Territorial units of that regiment. Its title was not changed. It retained the White Horse cap badge. Its links with West Kent remained unbroken. Yet it was the end of an era. The most apt way to end the story of that era is to quote some of the words spoken by The Duchess of Kent when she presented Colours to the battalion in 1956. On that occasion she said:

> "The spirit of voluntary service, upon which the 4th/5th Battalion was founded about a hundred years ago, is as much alive today as it was then. It is a spirit which has made this country respected throughout the world, and which we, in this county of Kent, are proud to possess in a high degree. I trust that this spirit will long be maintained."

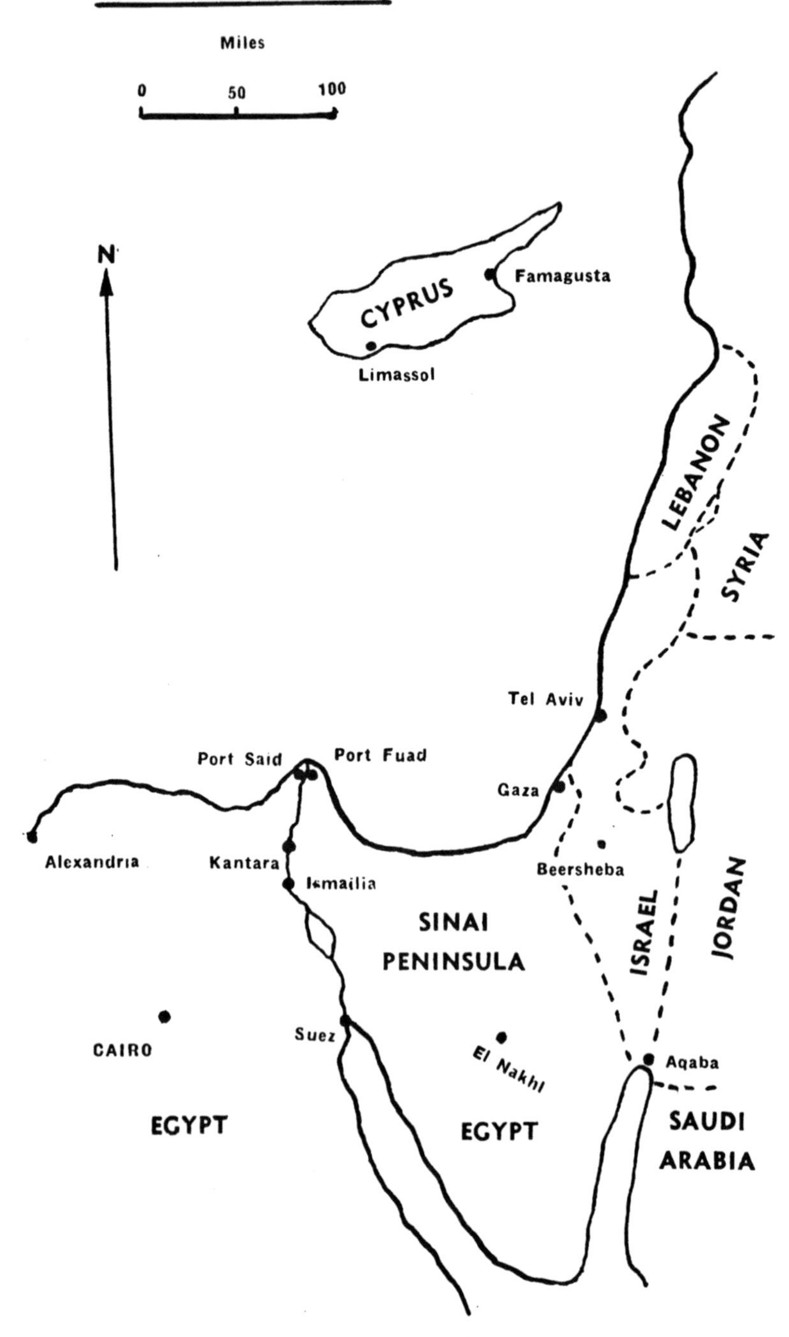
THE MIDDLE EAST
Miles
0
50
100
N
CYPRUS
Famagusta
Limassol
LEBANON
SYRIA
Tel Aviv
Port Said
Port Fuad
Gaza
Alexandria
Kantara
Ismailia
Beersheba
SINAI
PENINSULA
ISRAEL
JORDAN
Suez
CAIRO
El Nakhl
Aqaba
EGYPT
EGYPT
SAUDI
ARABIA

CHAPTER 4

The First Battalion in Egypt and Cyprus

November 1956 — September 1959

1. *The Situation in Egypt*

IN the autumn of 1947 the British Government announced that it intended to give up the Mandate in Palestine. On November 30 the United Nations Assembly passed a resolution proclaiming the establishment of the State of Israel as soon as the British Mandate ended. The Arab League, a loose organisation set up by the Arab nations in the Middle East, determined to destroy the State of Israel before it could be firmly established.

When the British withdrew from Palestine in May 1948, a full-scale war was in progress between the new State of Israel and the Arab League. The latter launched a series of attacks on Jewish settlers in the countryside and on Jewish inhabitants in the towns. The principal assailants were the Egyptian Army and the Arab Legion of Jordan. After several weeks of fighting, a United Nations resolution calling for a truce was accepted by both sides.

The first truce lasted for four weeks. There was a brief renewal of the fighting and, after ten days, another truce. When this broke down in October, Israel took the offensive. The Israelis thrust down the Sinai Peninsula, deep into Egyptian territory. Egypt sued for an armistice. This was signed at Rhodes in February 1949. Among its conditions was one which allowed Egypt to retain a narrow strip of coast near Gaza, known as the Gaza Strip. In the seven years that followed, the Arabs refused to convert the armistice into a general peace settlement. They denied the existence of the State of Israel, established an economic blockade against her and maintained that they were at war with her.

In the spring of 1956 the Egyptian Army began to train for a major assault on Israel. As part of the operation small detachments of Egyptian saboteurs, known as *fedayin*, made raids against outlying Israeli settlements and blew up a section of the Beersheba-Tel Aviv Railway. The Israelis retaliated. The reprisals were a warning to Egypt that Israel would hit back hard if attacked.

During October 1956 the *fedayin* raids increased in strength and frequency. Israel began partial mobilization on October 25. On the 27th the Israeli Cabinet issued a statement, which included the following: "The renewal of the activities of the *fedayin* by the Egyptian authorities in the last fortnight from Egyptian, Lebanese and Jordanian territory; the establishment of a military alliance, directed against Israel, between Egypt, Jordan and Syria; the declaration of the rulers of the Hashemite Kingdom that their principal concern is a war of destruction against Israel; the mobilization of Iraqi forces—all these developments have compelled us to mobilize a number of our reserves as a precautionary measure . . ."

The Israel Radio Service's nine o'clock news bulletin on the evening of October 29 began with this announcement: "Units of the Israel Defence Forces have penetrated and attacked *fedayin* bases . . . and have taken up positions to the west of the El Nakhl road junction on the approaches to the Suez Canal." On the 30th an Israeli parachute battalion was dropped in that area, and its patrols advanced to within 18 miles of the Suez Canal. On the northern side of the Sinai Peninsula a village seven miles from the Israeli border was captured. There was then a pause of 24 hours, during which the parachute battalion was reinforced by land.

It was during the pause on October 30 that the British and French Governments issued a requirement to Israel and Egypt:

(a) to cease hostilities by land, sea and air;

(b) to withdraw their troops ten miles from the Suez Canal;

(c) to allow Anglo-French forces to occupy Port Said, Ismailia and Suez so as to guarantee transit through the canal by ships of all nations;

(d) if one or both belligerents had not undertaken to comply within 12 hours, British and French forces would intervene.

The Israeli Government accepted the requirement provided that Egypt did the same. Egypt rejected it.

The Israelis resumed their attack on October 31. By November 2 they were masters of the Sinai Peninsula and had captured the Gaza Strip. The Egyptians had been put to flight, leaving tanks, guns and large quantities of equipment behind them. Not one Egyptian unit that was engaged made an organised withdrawal. In compliance with the Anglo-French requirement, the Israelis halted ten miles from the Suez Canal.

2. *The Suez Intervention*

The Anglo-French operation known as "Musketeer" was placed under the supreme command of General Sir Charles Keightley. The Land Task Force Commander was Lieutenant-General Sir Hugh Stockwell. General Keightley's orders were: to bring hostilities between Israel and Egypt to an end as soon as possible; to interpose his forces between those of Israel and Egypt; to occupy Port Said, Ismailia and Suez.

The British Land Forces at General Keightley's disposal were:

The 16th Independent Parachute Brigade in Cyprus.

The 3rd Commando Brigade Royal Marines in Malta.

The 6th Royal Tank Regiment in Malta.

The 3rd Infantry Division (less one brigade) in England.

The first task was to prevent the Egyptian Air Force from attacking the landing craft as they steamed from Malta along the Egyptian coast. So, at 4.15 p.m. on October 31, Valiant and Canberra bombers from Malta and Cyprus began to attack Egyptian military airfields. These attacks were continued with the aid of flares during the night.

From daylight on November 1, Allied aircraft carried out successful strikes on machines parked on nine Egyptian airfields. By the morning of the 2nd, the Egyptian Air Force had been virtually eliminated.

On the afternoon of the 2nd, the air attacks were switched to concentrations of vehicles and guns near Cairo. During the 3rd, other military targets were engaged, including the marshalling yard at Ismailia. The main effort on the 4th was directed against military movements on the roads leading to Port Said. Photographic reconnaissance showed that the Egyptians were prepared to defend Port Said and its beaches against a seaborne landing. It also disclosed that the Egyptians were blocking the Suez Canal, and sunken ships were seen in the entrance to Port Said harbour.

As a result of this information, General Keightley confirmed with his Task Force Commanders that an airborne assault on the Port Said area would be made on November 5.

Meanwhile the United Nations Assembly had decided to set up an Emergency Force to supervise a cease-fire, if that could be brought about. The British and French Governments welcomed the idea; they agreed to stop military action as soon as certain conditions had been fulfilled.

The morning of November 5 broke clear. At 5.15 a.m. British and French paratroopers from Cyprus, under Brigadier M. A. H. Butler, dropped about Port Said. The French, who made their jump to the south of the town, quickly secured the water works and the main bridges across the Interior Basin. The British 3rd Parachute Battalion Group, commanded by Lieutenant-Colonel Crook of The Queen's Own, dropped on El Gamil airfield just west of Port Said. With this battalion were three other Queen's Own officers—Captain Beale (B Company), Captain Howlett (Air Adjutant) and Lieutenant Newall (Machine Gun Platoon). Although they met with considerable small arms fire as they floated down, the British paratroopers captured the airfield in half an hour. They then advanced eastwards towards the town. The Egyptians fought stubbornly, the Coastguard Barracks being a particular centre of resistance.

In the afternoon, French paratroopers dropped on the southern outskirts of Port Fuad. During the evening there was a short cease-fire while terms of surrender were discussed. The Egyptian Government ordered the Military Commander of Port Said to fight on. When operations were resumed, the Egyptians distributed arms to civilians.

It became clear that Port Said could not be captured by the paratroopers alone, and that the seaborne force from Malta would have to make an opposed landing next morning (the 6th).

We must now trace the movements of the Vehicle Party of the 1st Battalion The Queen's Own. As recorded in Section 3 of Chapter 3, it had arrived in three groups in Malta. There, from October 10, the whole party lived in tents at the United Services Sports Club at Marsa. It consisted of Captain Osborne, 2nd Lieutenant Cannell, 2nd Lieutenant Hallidie and 84 other ranks. With it were 59 vehicles, 19 trailers and six 17-pounder anti-tank guns. In the vehicles were the three-inch mortars and the battalion's reserve of petrol, oil, ammunition and hard rations. While waiting for orders, embarkation in L.S.T.s was well rehearsed. At a briefing conference on October 25, instructions were issued for a full-scale loading exercise to take place on the 29th and 30th. As things turned out, this exercise was the start of the seaborne operation.

The "Musketeer" units and vehicle parties in Malta embarked and sailed in two convoys. The first, with which was the Assault Group of the 1st Battalion's Vehicle Party, consisted mainly of the Amphibious Warfare Squadron, Royal Navy (L.S.T.s and smaller landing craft); it left Malta on October 30. The second convoy, of three L.S.T.s, in one of which was the Follow-up Group of the 1st Battalion's Vehicle Party, sailed on the 31st. The weather was fine with a calm sea. It was not until November 4 that Captain Osborne, who was with the Assault Group, was told that the destination was Port Said, where assault landings were to be made on the 6th. The first convoy reached its destination exactly on time, the passage of over 900 miles having taken six days.

For 45 minutes before the seaborne landing, the beach at Port Said was subjected to covering fire from destroyers. Just before the leading troops reached the beach an air strike went in, setting fire to some huts on the lido. At 4.30 a.m. Royal Marine Commandos went ashore and across the beach in L.V.T.s (Landing Vehicles Tracked) before disembarking. They were followed by one squadron of the 6th Royal Tank Regiment. As the commandos moved inland, they came under fire from buildings on the sea front. They met considerable opposition in the town, but managed to link up with the French paratroopers south of Port Said. Later in the day reinforcements disembarked. All organised resistance ceased before dusk. By midnight, patrols had advanced some 25 miles southwards along the west bank of the Suez Canal.

That evening Sir Anthony Eden announced in the House of Commons that, pending confirmation that Egypt would accept the United Nations Emergency Force (U.N.E.F.), the British and French Governments were ordering their troops to cease fire unless they were attacked. British and French forces ceased fire at midnight on the 6th.

Having had a grandstand view of the seaborne landing, the Assault Group of the 1st Battalion's Vehicle Party disembarked from their L.S.T.s near the Casino Palace Hotel before 9 a.m. on the 6th. The vehicles were driven to the car park of a cinema, where slit trenches were dug. Some of the men helped the commandos to clear the neighbouring houses. Sniping went on for most of the day and night.

The Follow-up Group of the 1st Battalion's Vehicle Party landed at the Fish Market on November 7 and joined the Assault Group in the cinema. For the next few days the troops of the Vehicle Party made themselves generally useful by collecting arms and moving a large number of weapons from the main police station on the western edge of Port Said. Captain Osborne lent some Champs to the 3rd Parachute Battalion, which had taken over the area and was very short of vehicles for patrolling. News was received that the 3rd Infantry Division (less one brigade) was on its way, with the 1st Battalion in the van. With the help of Lieutenant-Colonel Crook, accommodation for the battalion was found in a school on the front near the Coastguard Barracks. The Vehicle Party moved from the cinema into the school to await the arrival of the main body.

On November 9 General Keightley was ordered to retain his hold on the Port Said area until the U.N.E.F. was established there. The British Land Forces were to be re-deployed as follows: the build-up of the 3rd Infantry Division (less one brigade) was to go on; the 6th Royal Tank Regiment was to remain in the area; the 3rd Commando Brigade was to return to Malta; the 16th Parachute Brigade was to be withdrawn.

It was on the morning of November 10 that the "Asturias", with the 1st Battalion and the Tactical Headquarters of the 3rd Infantry Division on board, entered Port Said harbour. The voyage, which had started at Southampton on the 2nd, had been uneventful except that,

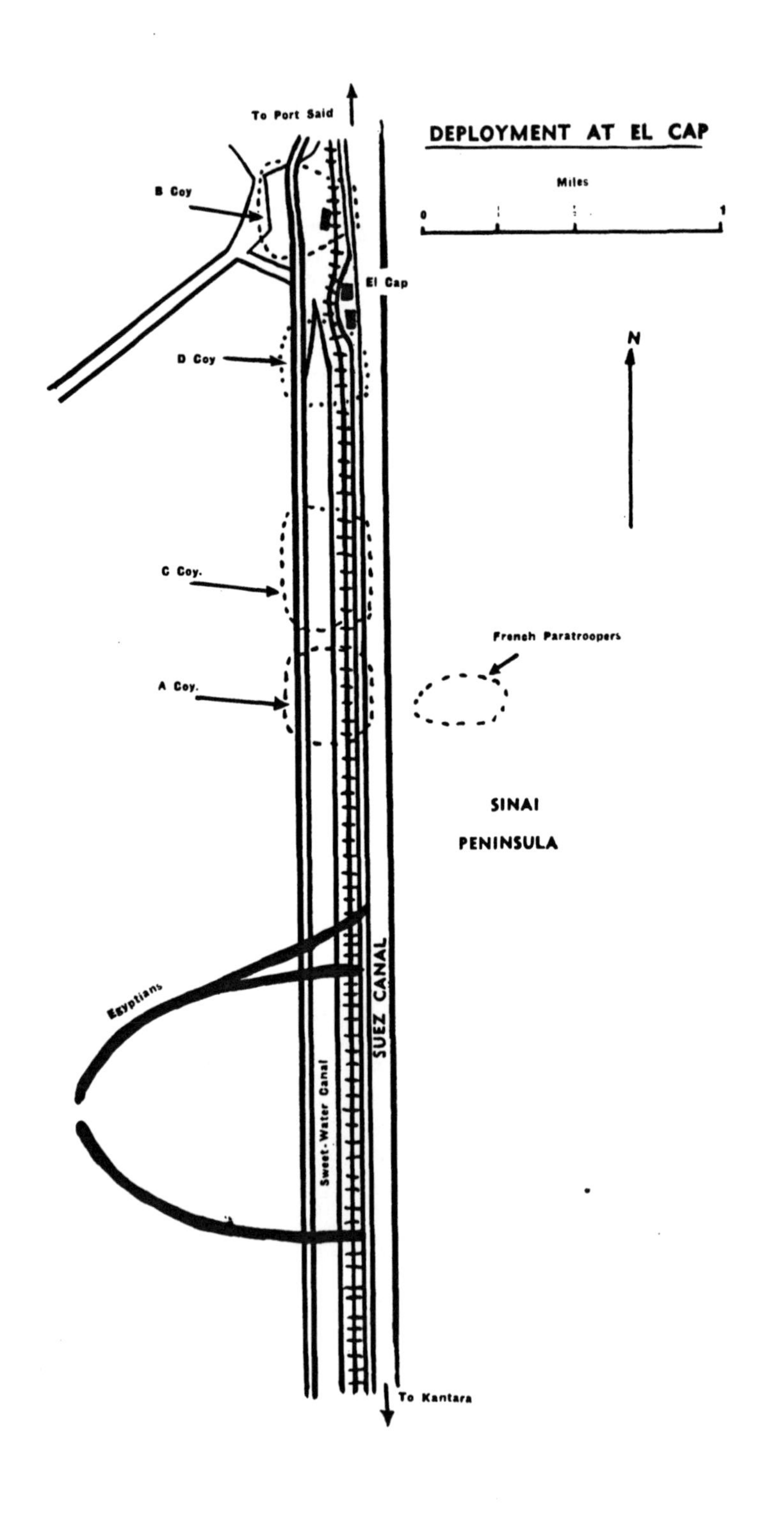
DEPLOYMENT AT EL CAP
Miles
0
1
To Port Said
B Coy
El Cap
D Coy
N
C Coy.
French Paratroopers
A Coy.
SINAI
PENINSULA
Egyptians
SUEZ CANAL
Sweet-Water Canal
To Kantara

after leaving Malta, a blackout of the ship had been ordered as a precaution against attacks by submarines. While the battalion was preparing to disembark, a Staff officer came aboard. He said that conditions in Port Said were still chaotic and sniping had stopped by day only; that our troops had consolidated a position on the west bank of the Suez Canal at El Cap, where The Queen's Own were to relieve the 2nd Parachute Battalion; that the commanding officer was to go at once to Brigadier Butler's Headquarters; and that the battalion was to go temporarily to the school, in which the Vehicle Party was already billeted.

The key personnel in the 1st Battalion were:

Comd. Officer	Lieutenant-Colonel P. C. M. Buckle.
2nd-in-Command	Major A. J. M. Flint, M.B.E.
Adjutant	Captain K. Dodson.
Quartermaster	Major A. G. Blake, M.B.E.
R.S.M.	W.O.I J. E. Grubb, M.B.E.
R.Q.M.S.	W.O.II G. V. I. Simpson.
O.C. H.Q. Company	Major T. V. Upton, M.B.E.
O.C. A Company	Major R. K. Dowse.
O.C. B Company	Major C. F. Willis, M.B.E., T.D.
O.C. C Company	Major R. Butler, M.B.E., M.C.
O.C. D Company	Major D. Monckton, M.C., T.D.
O.C. Support Company	Major M. R. Read, M.C.

A complete list of officers and warrant officers can be found in Appendix C.

Accompanied by Major-General J. B. Churcher (G.O.C. 3rd Infantry Division), Colonel Buckle and his Intelligence Officer went ashore in a launch. They were met by Captain Howlett. As they drove through the town in Queen's Own Champs, they were able to see some of the effects of the fighting. Many houses near the front were damaged. The Coastguard Barracks were a heap of rubble. The drains were overflowing, causing an evil smell. The Egyptians in the streets looked sullen and frightened. The shops were closed. Gone were the many vendors of souvenirs. Gone too were the sellers of dubious postcards.

At Parachute Brigade Headquarters, Brigadier Butler quickly

explained the situation. He and Colonel Buckle then left by helicopter for El Cap. Before they went Colonel Buckle asked Colonel Crook, who happened to be there, to take a warning order to Major Flint to the effect that the Reconnaissance Group was to be ready to move at 4 p.m. as the battalion would be taking over at El Cap at dawn next morning.

El Cap is some 25 miles south of Port Said. In 1956 it was a small village of wood and straw houses. There was a Canal Signal Station in it. During the flight southwards, the helicopter followed the line of the Suez Canal. On the left Colonel Buckle could see the Sinai Desert. Alongside the canal, and on the right of it, was a causeway. Side by side on the causeway were the canal road, a railway and a sweet-water canal. On the right of the causeway was a narrow strip of mud, on which another road, known as the Treaty Road, had been constructed. On the right of the Treaty Road were water and marsh. Several burnt-out Egyptian trucks, hit during low-level air attacks, were on both roads. Guns and tanks could be seen wherever there was any semblance of cover.

The 2nd Parachute Battalion was holding the El Cap position with one company forward in or about a belt of trees. This company occupied a frontage of some 200 yards from the Treaty Road on the right to the Suez Canal on the left. The Egyptians were in position on a horseshoe-shaped bund, which extended westwards from the Suez Canal for about 1,500 yards. Their frontage was nearly eight times as wide as the British. Their nearest posts were 800 yards away.

The Reconnaissance Group of the 1st Battalion moved up along the canal road in some Champs, a truck, and an Egyptian bus which had been commandeered. It arrived as darkness fell. The company commanders went into the El Cap Signal Station, which was to be the Battalion Headquarters, and Colonel Buckle gave out his orders. A Company was to take over the forward defended localities; C was to occupy a position on the causeway behind it; D was to be just forward of El Cap; and B was to take up positions to cover the right flank and rear of Battalion Headquarters. As the frontage was so narrow, the company localities would have to be practically one behind the other. The left flank on the eastern side of the Suez Canal was protected by paratroopers of the French Foreign Legion, who were under command. In support of the battalion were a troop of the 6th Royal Tank Regiment and a battery of 25-pounders.

After guides had led Major Dowse and the junior leaders of A Company to the forward positions, an Egyptian light machine gun opened fire on a fixed line up the Treaty Road. As this firing continued for some time, permission to retaliate was obtained. A burst of fire from the Vickers guns of the 2nd Parachute Battalion had an immediate effect on the Egyptians, who blazed away with every machine gun and rifle they possessed. The only casualty was Private Thompson, Major Dowse's batman, who was wounded in the back. A few more bursts from the Vickers guns ended the fusillade. The rest of the night was relatively quiet.

There was some anxiety that the take-over of the positions, which was carried out in daylight next morning, might cause more shooting. So, as the Egyptians were able to observe every movement, only small parties were allowed to go forward at a time. The relief went off without a hitch. The remainder of the day was spent in improving the defences, and collecting materials for revetting, camouflage and headcover. Some sporadic firing occurred during the night, but there were no more casualties.

The battalion remained at El Cap until November 21. The programme for each day was much the same. The troops worked in the hot sunshine, bathed in the Suez Canal, and tried to snatch a few hours' rest before the alarms that usually occurred at night. Rest was in fact almost impossible owing to the large number of visitors, who came from Port Said to see the front line. There were members of the Press of all nationalities, British and French generals, admirals, politicians, Staff officers of all the services, and naval sightseeing parties. A visitors' book was kept at Battalion Headquarters; about 60 names were written in it each day. Eventually the spectators were not allowed to go forward of El Cap. They were offered a view from the top of the Signal Station instead. Not many accepted it.

In spite of the constant interruptions, the defences became quite strong. A wire fence was erected across the front of A Company. An underground operations room was made at El Cap. The Intelligence Section plotted the Egyptian positions—with the unwitting co-operation of the Egyptians, who rose from their fox-holes in the mornings to shake their blankets.

If the cease-fire were broken and hostilities were resumed, the battalion had orders to attack within 24 hours and capture the bund and the dunes behind it. C Company was to lead the attack. This was a somewhat unpopular honour as the frontage was very narrow, the ground was flat, and an Egyptian minefield blocked the only possible route. The optimists who envisaged this assault hoped that a preliminary strike by the Fleet Air Arm would disperse the opposition.

Several Red Cross trains, conveying wounded Egyptians, passed through the lines. Those going southward to Cairo were driven by British crews as far as No-man's Land, where they were taken over by Egyptian crews. Those going northward were driven by Egyptian crews as far as No-man's Land, whence they were taken by British crews to Port Said. Captain Osborne, vigorously waving a white flag, supervised the change-over of crews.

Cover was so scanty in the El Cap area that most of the battalion's vehicles were sent back to B Echelon in the school in Port Said. There, the Quartermaster organised replenishments of rations, stores and canteen supplies. The padre, Father Norris from Buckfast Abbey, made many journeys in his Champ to bring sandbags from the quays to the front line. There was some concern about the Sweet-water Canal, the level of which was rapidly falling. After some time, an air photograph revealed that, while blowing a hole in the canal road, the Egyptians had breached this waterway as well. The damage was soon repaired.

The first United Nations Observers arrived on November 14. They drove down the Treaty Road from Port Said in their white saloon cars to No-man's Land, where Captain Osborne arranged for them to enter the Egyptian lines. Many men and women of the Press assembled to watch. The bodies of two journalists, a Frenchman and an American, who had been shot by the Egyptians when they drove too far down the canal road on the 10th, were handed over during the day.

Three British minesweepers swept the Suez Canal from Port Said on November 17. When they reached El Cap, the officers landed to visit Battalion Headquarters. Colonel Buckle received a message from a United Nations Observer that the Egyptian commander at Kantara was concerned about the movement of naval vessels and that, if they approached any closer, he would open fire. The flotilla commander said that he had finished his task. The minesweepers returned to Port Said, their mission completed.

The "Cymric", the slow ship bringing the battalion's Vickers machine guns and command vehicles, arrived that day. At last the whole unit was in Egypt. The guns were placed in positions which had already been prepared. The vehicles were very welcome, as for a week The Queen's Own had been providing transport for the two brigades of the 3rd Infantry Division, which had now disembarked.

On the 18th the Egyptians moved some troops to the east bank of the Suez Canal. The French accordingly decided to reinforce their positions there. While the activity was going on, the Egyptians opened fire from the bund. This caused a stir at the Allied headquarters in Port Said. Complaints were made to the United Nations Observers, and once more the front line was visited by numerous inquisitive journalists.

The advanced party of the 1st Battalion The Royal Fusiliers arrived at El Cap on the afternoon of November 20, and preparations for the hand-over began. Before the relief was completed on the 21st, 200 Norwegian troops of the U.N.E.F. passed through in a train on their way to Port Said. This was the first contingent of the Emergency Force to arrive. The crew of the train was as usual changed over in No-man's Land.

The battalion returned by road to Port Said, where it was billeted near the sea in flats, schools and a hospital. It was placed under the 19th Infantry Brigade for internal security duties and patrolling in the western end of the town. The arrival of United Nations troops had caused some demonstrations; two companies stood by to deal with any further disturbances. B Company—the Reservists—took over the guards on the electric power station and the gas works. One night one of this company's posts was sniped at. The fire was promptly returned by a burst from a Bren gun. There was no more shooting. The population in general was not openly antagonistic, but there was an underlying hostile element which was trying to make trouble.

At midnight on November 24, after the commanding officers of units had attended a conference held by General Keightley, the battalion received a warning order that it was to embark the next night in the "Dilwara". Now that the U.N.E.F. was assembling, a start was being made on the evacuation of British troops from Egypt. Later on Colonel Buckle was told that the destination was to be Cyprus, not England.

Before The Queen's Own embarked Sir Walter Monckton, who was in Port Said on a visit, and Lieutenant-General Sir Hugh Stockwell thanked all ranks for their good work. The troops were disappointed that they had not taken a more spectacular part in the operation, but were glad to know that their difficult task had been well done.

The embarkation took place in darkness on the night of November 25, in the presence of many journalists with their flashlights and cameras. Soon the "Dilwara" was slipping out of the harbour in a calm sea, taking The Queen's Own to further adventures. The vehicles and their drivers followed in L.S.T.s on the morning of the 26th.

After the battalion had gone, the U.N.E.F. gradually took over the positions on the Suez Canal. The last British and French troops withdrew from Port Said on December 22. Israel vacated the Gaza Strip in March 1957, and the Egyptians re-occupied the parts of their country from which they had been driven. A United Nations team undertook the clearance of the Suez Canal. The dispute between Israel and the Arab nations was no nearer a peaceful solution. But a large-scale war had been averted.

The General Service Medal with the clasp "Near East" was awarded to the officers and other ranks who took part in the Suez Intervention. Many of the 1st Battalion were already in possession of the medal and so received the clasp only.

3. *The Cyprus Emergency*

Although Cyprus has never been a part of Greece, the island was extensively colonized by the Greeks in ancient times. That is why four-fifths of the islanders speak Greek, share with Greece allegiance to the Eastern Orthodox Church, and think of themselves as Greek. This attachment to Greece caused them to desire union (Enosis) with that country. A minority of about 18 per cent. of the population of Cyprus is Turkish-speaking and Mohammedan in religion.

When, by an Anglo-Turkish convention, Britain took over from Turkey the administration of Cyprus in 1878, the Enosis movement was already flourishing. The Greek-Cypriots put their claim before the British Government, but to no avail. After the outbreak of war

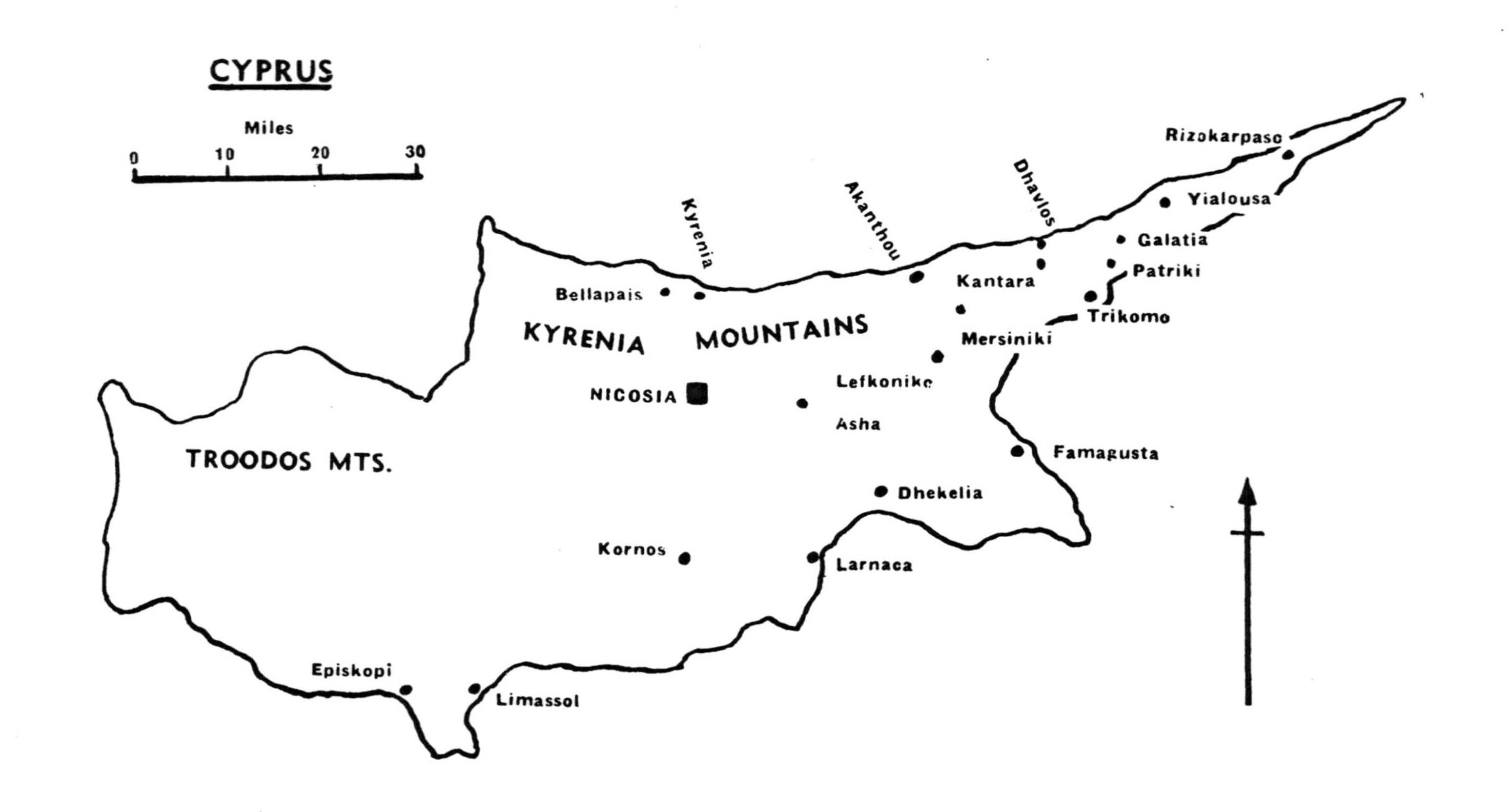
CYPRUS
Miles
0
10
20
30
Rizokarpaso
Yialousa
Galatia
Patriki
Trikomo
Dhavlos
Kantara
Mersiniki
Akanthou
Kyrenia
Bellapais
KYRENIA MOUNTAINS
NICOSIA
Lefkoniko
Asha
Famagusta
Dhekelia
Larnaca
Kornos
TROODOS MTS.
Episkopi
Limassol

between Britain and Turkey in 1914, Britain annexed Cyprus. In October 1915 Britain offered to cede the island to Greece on condition that the Greeks joined the Allies. The offer was refused. Cyprus remained in British hands and was proclaimed a Crown Colony in 1925. Thereafter the Enosis movement, led in the main by the dignitaries of the Orthodox Church of Cyprus, increased in strength.

After the 1939-1945 War the Ethnarch[1] took a delegation to London to ask for union with Greece. The British Government offered a new constitution instead. This was accepted by the Turkish members of the Consultative Assembly, but was rejected by the supporters of Enosis. The offer remained open. The Greek-Cypriot parties continued to affirm that to acquiesce in constitutional developments would be a betrayal of their aspirations. In January 1950 a plebiscite on Enosis, organised by the Orthodox Church of Cyprus, was conducted openly throughout the island. Over 95 per cent. of those entitled to go to the polls were said to have voted for union with Greece. Later in the year the Archbishop of Cyprus died. Makarios of Citium was elected to succeed him at the early age of 37. The new Ethnarch soon became a forceful leader in the struggle for Enosis.

From the British point of view Cyprus was of considerable importance. Since the development of air-power the island had become a strategic centre in the Middle East. Britain had treaty obligations to some of the nearby Arab States. She was vitally interested in the southern flank of the North Atlantic Treaty Organisation. She shared with other members of that organisation, including Greece and Turkey, obligations for the air and naval defence of the Eastern Mediterranean. She considered that Cyprus was essential as a base from which these responsibilities could be discharged. Indeed, in August 1954 the British Government announced that the headquarters of the Middle East Command were to be transferred from the Suez Canal Zone to the island.

The positions maintained by the leaders of the Enosis movement on the one side, and the British Government on the other, were irreconcilable. An added complication was that the Turkish minority was firmly opposed to union with Greece. It seemed that a peaceful solution could not be found.

Colonel Grivas, an officer in the Greek Army, landed illegally

[1]Ethnarch, meaning the "leader of the nation," is the traditional title of the Archbishop of Cyprus.

in Cyprus in November 1954 to be the military commander of the Enosis movement. He began to organise EOKA (National Organisation of Cypriot Fighters). The personnel were taught first aid and how to use small arms, time-bombs, grenades, ground and cover. Arms were smuggled into the island in Greek ships. Bands of guerrillas, normally wearing military boots, riding breeches and pullovers, were organised to operate near the villages in the mountains. In the villages themselves groups of young people, mostly unarmed, were trained as agents. A system of couriers, by which Grivas could keep in touch with his area commanders, was arranged. Codes were evolved for the transmission of orders by telephone and through the post. EOKA had its own cars, with a pool of drivers.

About a third of Cyprus is mountainous. In the centre of the island are the Troodos Mountains. Nearly 50 miles in length and with an average width of 20 miles, they consist of a bewildering confusion of peaks, interspersed by deep, wooded ravines. Extending along the north coast for 75 miles is the narrow Kyrenia mountain range. It is generally low, but contains many rocky slopes; the narrow tracks are steep, often with a precipitous drop on one side.

In these two ranges EOKA constructed many hides. Some of them were on slopes, others in dry gullies or in caves. All were in unexpected and more or less inaccessible places. There were hides in the villages too, behind the chimney of a house or in a cellar concealed by jars of wine. In order to prevent the hides from being discovered, Grivas laid down strict rules concerning footprints and litter; no open fires were to be lit; no lights were to be shown at night. Pepper was strewn round the hides so that dogs would not be able to detect them.

Terrorism, organised by EOKA, began on April 1, 1955. In the early hours of that morning a series of explosions occurred in the principal towns of Cyprus, causing damage to Government buildings, military installations and police stations. Simultaneously a proclamation, cyclostyled on one sheet of paper, was distributed all over the island. It urged the Cypriots to prove themselves worthy of their Greek forefathers, and ended with the slogan: "Forward together for the liberty of Cyprus!" At its foot were the Greek letters EOKA. This was a call for armed action.

The British Government announced that it reserved the right to take any counter-measures that were necessary to safeguard Cypriot and British lives. The counter-measures actually taken included the imposition of curfews and a ban on processions. Even so, bomb explosions, injuries to British servicemen, and demonstrations continued. Towards the end of November Field-Marshal Sir John Harding, who had arrived on October 3 to take up his appointment as Governor, proclaimed a State of Emergency, made necessary by an increase in terrorist outrages. By the end of 1955, the 10,000 British troops in Cyprus were being used for riot-breaking and search operations. Archbishop Makarios, who was believed to be personally involved in the EOKA campaign, was deported to the Seychelles Islands on March 9, 1956,

The exile of the Ethnarch caused an increase in violence. Sir John Harding took vigorous counter-measures. Military operations were carried out in the hills in an endeavour to capture the guerrillas. A reward was offered for information that led to the arrest of Grivas. All Cypriot citizens were ordered to carry identity cards. But the murder of a Turkish policeman caused Turkish-Cypriot attacks on Greek-Cypriot property, with a consequent increase in communal tension.

After Colonel Nasser nationalised the Suez Canal in July 1956, more British troops were sent to Cyprus. Intensive drives against the terrorists gradually met with greater success. Extended curfews, lasting for as long as a week, with breaks for shopping, were imposed. These curfews created much resentment among the population and brought retaliation from EOKA. Early in November four British servicemen were killed. During the following three days, 14 murders occurred. Altogether, there were 416 acts of violence that November, the month of the Suez Intervention.

This was the situation when the 1st Battalion entered the turbulent arena.

4. *The 1st Battalion Arrives in Cyprus*

The troopship "Dilwara" arrived off Limassol on November 27, 1956. The 1st Battalion disembarked in lighters and went by road to Dhekelia, which is on the south coast near Larnaca. At Dhekelia The Queen's Own occupied a tented camp, while their future was decided.

On December 5 the camp was visited by the Director of Operations, Major-General D. A. Kendrew, who spoke first to the officers and then to all ranks. He told them that they were to remain in Cyprus for three years, the first 12 months of which would be in a "non-family area". The battalion was to be part of the 51st Independent Infantry Brigade Group, which was commanded by Brigadier J. A. R. Robertson. The formation sign would be a Black Swan.

While waiting for the move to the operational area, the troops carried out some internal security training. A few patrols were sent out. D Company erected a camp about a mile away from the rest of the unit and mounted guard there over the vehicles of "Musketeer" units withdrawn from Egypt. Major Read departed to take up a Staff appointment in Korea; Major Upton was transferred from H.Q. Company to command the Support Company. Major Willis left to be seconded to The Gold Coast Regiment. Some British Self-loading Rifles were issued to replace Lee-Enfields. On December 22 the Reservists, the Deferred Regulars and a National Service Group embarked at Limassol for the United Kingdom. After they had gone, the battalion was some 350 under strength, B Company being reduced to Company Headquarters only.

The advanced party moved up to the Karpas Peninsula, in the north-east of the island, on December 27 to take over from the 1st Battalion The Highland Light Infantry. The main body followed on January 3, 1957. Three platoons were temporarily left at Dhekelia to guard the "Musketeer" vehicles and to hand in camp stores.

5. *The Karpas Peninsula*

The Karpas Peninsula is known as "The Panhandle" because of the shape of the island. Extending for most of its length is the eastern part of the Kyrenia mountain range. The 1st Battalion's operational area, which covered about 350 square miles, included the whole peninsula. Battalion Headquarters, H.Q. Company and D Company were in a camp at Dhavlos on the north coast. C Company was at Kantara, some four miles inland. A Company was in the neck of the peninsula at a place called Mersiniki. The Support Company was in three camps, two near Yialousa and one at Rizokarpaso, towards the north-eastern end of "The Panhandle".

In the early stages of the terrorist campaign the Karpas Peninsula had been the EOKA training ground. In January 1957 it was generally considered that there were no large bands of guerrillas in the mountains of the peninsula, but that there were numerous EOKA agents in the many villages. To find them, without some information as to their whereabouts, was hard work and required much patience. Information was forthcoming only from the police. Since the Special Branch representative responsible for the area lived in Famagusta, 30 miles from Dhavlos, liaison with him was difficult. There were police stations, under the charge of police sergeants, in only three of the villages in the peninsula.

For the first few weeks, most of the troops were occupied in reconnoitring the area. EOKA leaflets and banners were found in some of the villages. A big effort was made to improve the camps, which required a considerable amount of work to bring them up to standard. On January 11 Mr. John Hare, the Secretary of State for War, unexpectedly arrived at Dhavlos in a helicopter. He brought the news that married personnel could be granted 28 days' leave in the United Kingdom in order to attend to their domestic affairs. He also visited C Company at Kantara.

During February and March, several bombs and shot-guns were found in the area, mainly by the Support Company. Some shots were fired into the camp at Kantara. A number of bombs were thrown at the battalion's vehicles, but only once were there any serious casualties or damage. On that occasion, on February 5, a bomb exploded under the vehicle in which Major Butler was travelling. He was wounded in the right leg. His driver, Private Mills, was slightly injured. They were evacuated to the military hospital in Nicosia, and later Major Butler was flown to England. Following this incident C Company cordoned and searched a village near Kantara, but without result. Captain Shearburn replaced Major Butler in command of C Company.

In a tragic accident on March 3, Private Martin of A Company was shot in the chest at Mersiniki Camp. He was buried in the military cemetery at Nicosia on the 5th.

Four Greener guns and their ammunition were stolen from the police station at Rizokarpaso on March 5. These weapons were apparently taken by EOKA terrorists, aided by a disloyal policeman. Although The Queen's Own were not responsible for them, the battalion sealed "The Panhandle" by road blocks for 24 hours while searches were made. The guns were not recovered. A system of rewards was started in the unit for successful searching. Inquisitive patrolling made up for lack of information, and arms, ammunition or warlike materials were discovered nearly every day.

Two short operations were carried out in March. In the first, D Company and the Support Company cordoned and searched the secondary schools at Yialousa and Rizokarpaso; EOKA leaflets and a duplicating machine were found. In the second, six Greek-Cypriots were arrested in their houses at Rizokarpaso in the early hours of the morning. They were thought by the police to be members of the village EOKA group.

Field-Marshal Sir John Harding visited the battalion on March 8. At Dhavlos he inspected the Quarter Guard and spoke to all available personnel. He then flew eastwards to see the Support Company.

Major Flint, who had been acting commanding officer during the absence on duty of Lieutenant-Colonel Buckle, was appointed to command the battalion as from March 31. Major Archer became 2nd-in-command. R.S.M. Grubb had received a commission and was now Transport Officer. C.S.M. Parker had been promoted to R.S.M.

After Grivas had announced in a leaflet that he would suspend operations so as to facilitate the resumption of negotiations between Britain and Archbishop Makarios, the British Government decided to release the Ethnarch from his detention. He would not, however, be allowed to return to Cyprus for the time being. The Archbishop arrived in Athens from his exile in the Seychelles Islands on April 17.

The news that the Ethnarch was to be released was greeted with jubilant demonstrations in Cyprus. For some months the island returned to something nearer normality. Acts of violence by EOKA virtually ceased, though leaflets continued to be issued by Grivas and slogans still appeared on walls in the villages. A number of the restrictions were relaxed. The main towns were placed in bounds for the troops, who no longer had to carry arms when off duty. Vehicles need not be escorted.

After the tension of the previous three months, all ranks were able to enjoy a little recreation, particularly swimming. The Karpas

Peninsula, which had been a restricted area, was open to all, and British and Cypriot families came in large numbers to the pleasant beaches for picnics and bathing parties. British minesweepers often anchored in Dhavlos Bay, while some of the sailors came ashore to visit The Queen's Own. Combined Services Entertainments (C.S.E. Shows) were given in the theatre in Dhavlos Camp, the casts sometimes staying overnight at the Regina Hotel, Kantara.

Lieutenant-Colonel Flint altered the routine in the 1st Battalion to suit the more peaceful situation. One platoon only in each company carried out operations; another platoon trained for the future; the third performed guards and fatigues in camp. The roles were changed over each week.

Internal security operations continued in "The Panhandle", though on a smaller scale. The aim was to prevent EOKA from reorganising for further outbreaks of terrorism. The dress for these operations depended on the weather; typically it was: beret, pullover, denim trousers, rubber-soled boots, web equipment and rucksack. Patrols occasionally found items of warlike equipment. A number of Cypriots, caught in the act of painting slogans on walls, were detained. Some people were arrested for distributing leaflets in the villages.

Training included the use of helicopters for dropping troops into difficult country by rope. Much time was devoted to the improvement of snapshooting at moving targets. The signallers were given practice in communicating with widespread detachments. A cadre course for N.C.O.s was held at Dhavlos.

Corporal O'Gorman, the M.T. N.C.O. with A Company, was killed on July 6, when his Land Rover overturned on the road between Trikomo and Famagusta. He was buried on the 8th in the military cemetery at Nicosia.

During the summer several villages were cordoned and searched, notably Patriki, which had been a centre of trouble, intrigue and hostility. Major Monckton[1] was usually in charge of these operations. On October 9, Dhavlos itself was searched. All males in the village were placed in a cage, where they were screened by the police. Six Greek-Cypriots, suspected to be members of EOKA, were arrested.

Dr. Kutchuk, the Turkish-Cypriot leader, addressed a political meeting at a village called Galatia on October 13. Tactical Head-

[1]Nephew of Sir Walter Monckton.

quarters and D Company were sent there so as to be at hand to deal with any disturbances. No incidents occurred.

The whole battalion was deployed on internal security duties on October 28, the anniversary of Italy's abortive attack on Greece in 1940. During the day there were processions and assemblies in the villages in "The Panhandle", leaflets were distributed and many slogans were painted on walls. The only serious incident in the battalion was when a patrol of C Company had to intervene to rescue a policeman. A soldier of a neighbouring unit was attacked in a village and lost his rifle; D Company helped to cordon the village but the rifle was not recovered.

Throughout the hot weather, bathing was the main recreation. In order to improve the standard of swimming in the battalion, an association known as the "Rock Club" was formed. To qualify as a Class A member a man had to swim to an isolated rock about 1,500 yards from the Dhavlos shore and, after a short rest, back to land. Class B members were those who swam out to the rock but returned by boat. Most of the Class A members were sergeants. An Inter-Company Aquatics Competition, organised by Captain Neve, was won by H.Q. Company.

The Middle East Motor Cycle Trial was held in Malta in August. The Queen's Own team was second, only one point behind the Cyprus District Workshops, R.E.M.E. In the Brigade Assault-at-Arms (a marathon contest which included the firing of all weapons and competitions in platoon tactical handling, signalling, stretcher-bearing, voice-procedure, and driving and maintenance of vehicles) the battalion stretcher-bearers and signallers were first and second respectively.

A farewell parade for Sir John Harding at Famagusta on October 26 was attended by the commanding officer, the adjutant and a representative from each company. The new Governor, Sir Hugh Foot, arrived in Cyprus on December 3.

The move from the Karpas Peninsula began on November 1, when the advanced party left Dhavlos and went to the Cyprus Broadcasting Service (C.B.S.) Camp near Nicosia. The various companies followed at intervals. The move was completed on the 19th. By then, some of the families had arrived from England. As married quarters were scarce in Nicosia, most of them had to occupy private accommodation.

6. *The Island Reserve*

C.B.S. Camp was on the Limassol road about two miles from Nicosia. It was a tented camp with huts for the messes, the dining hall, the cookhouse, the institutes and the stores, As usual in Cyprus, the perimeter was protected by barbed-wire. The camp was in need of repair and repainting, and paving stones had to be laid to make paths in readiness for the winter rains. The great advantage was that the battalion was concentrated, which made the organisation of training and the raising of teams for games much easier.

In its new station the battalion was part of the 3rd Independent Infantry Brigade, commanded by Brigadier J. A. J. Read. This brigade was the Island Mobile Reserve, whose task was to fight terrorist gangs in any part of Cyprus, should EOKA again become active. As the majority of the operations were likely to be in the Troodos Mountains, all companies were sent in turn to the Troodos area for short periods of training.

After Christmas, which the married men celebrated with their families, the personnel of the Battalion and Company Headquarters took part in a Brigade Signal Exercise in the Larnaca area. This was followed by a Brigade Internal Security Scheme in the Troodos Mountains, the whole battalion being deployed. At the end of this scheme snow began to fall in the hills, and the troops just got clear of the area before the roads became icy. Next day there were six feet of snow in the Troodos Mountains.

At the end of January 1958 the Turkish-Cypriots, believing that their interests were being largely disregarded in the political struggle, organised demonstrations in the principal towns of Cyprus. These demonstrations, which had to be broken up by police using tear-gas, developed into dangerous riots. Clashes occurred with the Security Forces as well as with Greek-Cypriots. On the 27th, rioting became serious in Nicosia. Troops were stoned. Police and firemen were injured. Greek-Cypriot property was destroyed. On the morning of the 28th, the 1st Battalion was placed at one hour's notice to move into the town in support of the police. But the Turkish-Cypriot leaders appealed for calm, and rioting ceased by mid-day all over the island. Order had been restored for the time being. In these riots seven Turkish-Cypriots lost their lives.

While the situation remained quiet, the battalion was able to concentrate on training, shooting and sport. Two companies at a time were normally in the mountains on minor tactical training. There was a Brigade Exercise which began near Famagusta and ended in "The Panhandle". All ranks took part with enthusiasm in football, hockey, boxing and athletics competitions. The outstanding sporting event was the Cyprus District Rugby Cup Final, in which The Queen's Own lost to the 1st Battalion The Welch Regiment by five points to nine after a very hard game. At shooting there were two successes: the Machine Gun Platoon won the Army Rifle Association Machine Gun Cup (Overseas), and the battalion team was runner-up for the Middle East Battle Trophy.

Greek Independence Day was celebrated by the Cypriots on March 25. The Security Forces were held in readiness throughout the island to deal with any rioting. The 1st Battalion was sent to the Famagusta area. While the platoons of A and C Companies stood by in the police stations of six villages, the rest of the battalion bivouacked in a pleasant camp near the sea. No disturbances occurred, and the troops returned to C.B.S. Camp in the evening.

Exasperated by the lack of progress in the political negotiations, EOKA resumed its attacks on the Security Forces. The terrorists also attacked, and often murdered, those Greek-Cypriots whom they believed to be traitors. In the middle of May, information was received that Grivas might be conducting this campaign from a hide north of Limassol. A cordon was thrown round the area by some units of the Island Reserve, the troops involved being ordered to remain in position until the hide was found or Grivas made a break for want of food. On June 7, the 1st Battalion was ordered to prepare to take part in this operation.

Before the battalion moved out, the Turkish-Cypriots struck again. Shouting "Partition or Death!" they attacked Greek-Cypriots in all the major towns on the island. In Nicosia on June 8 nearly 1,000 of them advanced on the Greek sector, yelling anti-Greek slogans. The alarm was given by ringing the church bells. The Security Forces were prepared. Two thousand British troops intervened by patrolling the wire fence which separated the two sectors. Even so, by the time order was restored 59 Greek-Cypriots were casualties. Once again The Queen's Own were under notice to move into Nicosia but were not required.

Next day the battalion left C.B.S. Camp for the Limassol area, where it spent five interesting days in the cordon round the place in which Grivas was thought to be hiding. It then returned to Nicosia to erect camps for the 1st Guards Brigade, which was on its way from England. Grivas—if he was ever there—managed to get away unscathed.

On July 1 the whole Island Reserve set out for the Paphos Forest in the Troodos Mountains, where terrorists were said to be lurking. The battalion was divided into two task forces, A and C Companies being commanded by Colonel Flint, and D and the Support Companies by Major Archer. The operation began with helicopters landing groups to establish observation posts round the area. Patrolling and searching were then carried out by day. Ambushes and listening posts were placed in position at night. As there seemed to be no EOKA guerrillas in the vicinity, the brigade returned to base on the 3rd.

A week later information was received concerning a hide used by Kyriakos Matsis, 2nd-in-command to Grivas. The hide was on a steep ridge of the Kyrenia Range, overlooking Akanthou in the Karpas Peninsula. Against it, the Island Reserve launched an operation on July 10. For the first three days the battalion cordoned and searched villages west of Akanthou, so as to divert the attention of the guerrillas from the suspected area. Road blocks were placed on all the roads. At 4.15 a.m. on the 13th, ten helicopters flew from Nicosia, alighted on a landing zone near Brigade Headquarters and began to lift 87 men of The Queen's Own and 120 of the 45th Commando Royal Marines to establish a cordon round the hide. The rest of the battalion moved in vehicles along bumpy roads and mountain tracks to thicken the cordon. When the cordon was complete, a detachment of the 3rd Grenadier Guards searched the hide. It was empty, and looked as though it had not been used for some time. After a thorough search had been made and no terrorists had been found, the operation was called off. The battalion returned to C.B.S. Camp on the 20th, having had little sleep for 11 nights.

A determined effort was then made to round-up EOKA agents and village groups all over the island. Road blocks were placed simultaneously on all the main and most of the subsidiary roads. At the road blocks, identity cards were checked. Many Cypriots were arrested; in fact the number of people detained was higher than had been expected. For this operation, the battalion was sent to the Limassol area for ten days. It had the satisfaction of detaining, with the help of the police, well over 100 suspects.

In August, part of the Island Reserve was sent to search three villages on the Famagusta road which were known to contain strong EOKA groups. The village of Asha, 13 miles west of Nicosia, was allotted to The Queen's Own, who threw a cordon round it before daylight on August 2. On the first morning all males in the village between ten and 65 years of age were placed in a cage, where they were screened by officers of the Special Branch. About 25 wanted men were arrested. One of them disclosed a cache, in which were four pipe-bombs. On the 4th, a former member of the village EOKA group identified 87 individuals who had connections with EOKA. They were detained in the cage for questioning. For ten more days, three companies maintained the cordon while the rest of the battalion searched the houses, the backyards and the manure heaps of Asha. D Company found two other pipe-bombs under the tiled floor of an unoccupied house, and some masks, cloaks, megaphones and other EOKA equipment in a pile of manure. The drummers discovered five bombs in an outhouse. On the evening of the 14th those individuals in the cage, who were not wanted by the police, were released; the troops were conveyed back to C.B.S. Camp.

For the next 12 weeks The Queen's Own were employed, in turn with two other units, on guard duties in Nicosia and its vicinity, with one company on internal security duties in Famagusta. The normal routine was one week on duty, one week standing-by, and one week on training. The places guarded by the battalion in Nicosia included three detention camps and the Central Prison.

During those 12 weeks the political situation in Cyprus deteriorated. An EOKA leaflet distributed at the end of August called for passive resistance and a boycott of British goods. Bomb explosions in N.A.A.F.I. shops in the first half of September were followed by a wave of terrorism in Nicosia. There was a 24-hour strike on September 30. The murder of Mrs. Cutcliffe, the wife of a British serviceman, in Famagusta on October 3 caused the imposition of a rigid curfew and the rounding-up of all males in the vicinity of the crime. To combat these new forms of violence, arms were distributed to British civilians. Over 4,000 Cypriots were dismissed from employment at the R.A.F. base at Episkopi and in N.A.A.F.I. canteens.

The Queen's Own staged a demonstration of fire power and anti-ambush drill on October 22. It was watched by a large number of spectators, including members of the Press. At the end of it the

GUARD OF HONOUR MOUNTED BY A COMPANY OF THE 1ST BATTALION AT EPISKOPI, 27TH NOVEMBER, 1958.

new Director of Operations, Major-General K. T. Darling, explained that it showed clearly his policy for dealing with EOKA ambushes.

In November the battalion was widely dispersed. A Company went to Episkopi for ten days to provide two Guards of Honour, one for the outgoing C.-in-C. Middle East Air Forces and the other for his successor. Both guards, wearing No. 1 Dress, were commanded by Captain Clarke; Lieutenant Colgate carried the Regimental Colour. C and D Companies, under Captain Norton, were in the West Larnaca area for three weeks. Platoons guarded three police stations. With the help of tracker dogs a score of Greek-Cypriots, who were suspected of acts of violence, were arrested. Three bombs and a pistol were found in Kornos. Sergeant Scudder was slightly injured when a ration truck was ambushed. The Support Company (Major H. B. H. Waring) was in the Kyrenia area from November 6 till December 7. Its first task was to cordon Ayios Yeoryios, where an important EOKA leader, Andreas Sophocleous, was captured in a well and some arms and ammunition were discovered. The company then threw a cordon round Bellapais and maintained a curfew on its inhabitants for 19 days. The whole EOKA group in this village was detained; the Machine Gun Platoon found ten bombs and some leaflets in a cave.

While the Support Company was at Bellapais, the 1st Wiltshires killed Kyriakos Matsis in a hide beneath the paved floor of a house in Dhikomo, a village only a few miles south of Bellapais.

On December 2 The Queen's Own, less the Support Company, reinforced the troops in the Kyrenia area. For five days they searched a number of villages west of Bellapais. Several suspects were arrested, but no weapons or explosives were found. The entire battalion returned to C.B.S. Camp on the 7th.

The last Island Reserve operation, in which The Queen's Own, as a whole, took part, was in "The Panhandle". On the night of December 9, A Company moved in on Akanthou across the hills on foot, while the rest of the battalion approached by road. A cordon was established round the village. All males between 14 and 60 years of age were screened by members of the Special Branch. Nine Greek-Cypriots were arrested. C Company found a big EOKA hide under a house. In it were a large quantity of explosives, a shot-gun, two shells and an aerial bomb. Nothing else was discovered in spite of diligent searching, and the battalion moved south to assist the 3rd

Grenadier Guards in a search of the town of Lefkoniko. This larger operation was well co-ordinated. Apart from a number of important arrests, there were no immediate results. The Queen's Own were back in camp for Christmas.

On Christmas Eve an EOKA leaflet was circulated in Cyprus. It said that EOKA would cease activities on condition that the British did the same. Sir Hugh Foot pointed out that he had already promised that, as soon as it was apparent that violence had ended for good, the task could begin of bringing the emergency to a conclusion. Part of the Island Reserve carried out a clearing-up operation in the Troodos Mountains and a signal exercise in the north-east of the island. The Governor denied that these were a breach of the truce.

7. *The End of the Emergency*

In an effort to find a final settlement to the Cyprus problem, conversations were held between the Greek and Turkish Governments at the end of 1958. The British Government gave its full support, declaring that so long as British bases were retained it was prepared to consider the transfer of sovereignty over the rest of the island. On February 5, 1959, negotiations began in Zurich between the Prime Ministers and Foreign Ministers of Greece and Turkey. These negotiations ended on the 11th with an agreement on the outline of a scheme for a settlement. The two Foreign Ministers then flew to London to discuss the Zurich Agreement with the British Government. A conference, in which Archbishop Makarios and Dr. Kutchuk took part, was convened at Lancaster House on the 17th. The London Agreements were initialled on the 19th. They included: the Formation of a Republic of Cyprus; a Treaty of Guarantee between the Republic of Cyprus and the United Kingdom, Greece and Turkey; a Treaty of Alliance between the Republic of Cyprus, Greece and Turkey; and an Article guaranteeing the integrity of two base areas under the sovereignty of the United Kingdom. The two sovereign base areas were to be at Episkopi and Dhekelia.

Sir Hugh Foot took immediate steps to bring about a return to normal conditions in Cyprus. He withdrew the existing emergency regulations, including the detention and restriction of movement of individuals; revoked the deportation order against Archbishop Makarios; and announced amnesty terms and arrangements for the safe-conduct to Greece of Grivas and anyone he wished to take with him. The Ethnarch returned to Cyprus on March 1. Grivas left the island and returned to Athens on the 17th.

After the London Agreements had been initialled, the role of The Queen's Own changed. They left the Island Reserve on February 23 and came under command of the 50th Independent Infantry Brigade. A farewell ceremonial parade was held in honour of Brigadier Read, the Queen's Colour being carried by Lieutenant Champion and the Regimental by 2nd Lieutenant Whitty. Before the march past Brigadier Read made a stirring speech, in which he praised the battalion very highly for its efficient work during the past 15 months. After the parade he drove to the sergeants' mess, where he was presented with a crib board shaped like a rifle butt.

The task of the 50th Brigade was to maintain internal security in Nicosia and the surrounding rural area. It was commanded by Brigadier D. W. Lister, formerly of The Lancashire Fusiliers. The units in the brigade were the 1st Suffolks, the 1st Lancashire Fusiliers, the 43rd Light Anti-Aircraft Regiment and The Queen's Own. Each unit was responsible for a sector of the Nicosia Rural Area; the sector allotted to The Queen's Own was to the north-east of the town. Each unit in turn took over for a month the internal security duties in Nicosia itself, including the guards over government establishments.

It soon became abundantly clear to the troops that the military as well as the political situation had changed. The day after D Company took over guard duties at two detention camps some eight miles from Nicosia, the gates were thrown open and the detainees were allowed to go free. When the political prisoners were released from the Central Prison, C Company had to watch them being greeted as heroes by the population. The battalion merely stood by while thousands of Greek-Cypriots moved into Nicosia to welcome back Archbishop Makarios. Wanted men, whom the Security Forces had been seeking for months, openly wore EOKA uniform in the streets. These things were difficult for the average soldier to stomach. So was the glorification of Grivas on his departure. Even worse was the provocation by Cypriot youths of the troops when they were out in town. This sometimes led to fights. The Queen's Own had to provide foot patrols in the Nicosia area to help the Military Police to deal with these incidents.

These minor troubles gradually ceased. In April, for the first time for many months, the battalion was free of all guards and commitments. For the Security Forces the emergency was deemed to be at an end on April 18.

The qualification for the "Cyprus" clasp to the General Service Medal was 120 days' consecutive service in Cyprus between April 1, 1955, and April 18, 1959.

The battalion did well in the inter-unit sporting competitions in the early months of 1959. The cross-country and athletics teams were both placed 4th. The boxers were beaten in the semi-final by the 29th Field Regiment, who ultimately won the trophy. In the seven-a-side Rugby competition the team reached the final. The Rugby XV gained a notable success by winning the Cyprus Army Cup; they beat The Royal Welch Fusiliers in the final by five points to three. For these achievements The Queen's Own were awarded the Palestine Commemoration Cup, which was held for 12 months by the unit with the best sporting record in Cyprus during the past year.

8. *The Last Months in Cyprus*

Now that the emergency was over, the battalion adopted practically a peacetime routine of training, classification on the ranges, physical efficiency tests, ceremonial parades and sport. Each company in turn moved out to camps in the Troodos Mountains or near the west coast for section and platoon training. In the early mornings, before the heat of the day, the troops carried out tests to prepare them for the re-introduction of Star Grading for higher rates of pay. A course was held for junior N.C.Os. The officers took part in T.E.W.T.s and Officers' Days. There were some battalion and brigade exercises.

Beating Retreat by the corps of drums of The Parachute Regiment and the massed bands of The Black Watch, The Royal Ulster Rifles, The Argyll and Sutherland Highlanders, The Durham Light Infantry, The Queen's Own and the Cyprus Police took place in the Moat, Nicosia, by floodlight on the nights of April 29 and 30. Major H. B. H. Waring organised the ceremony. The bands were conducted by Mr. Watkins, and the parade was led by Drum-Major Clark; they were the senior bandmaster and drum-major in Cyprus. His Excellency the Governor congratulated all those who took part on a brilliant display.

The Queen's Birthday was celebrated on June 13. The parade in the Moat, Nicosia, was watched by officers and sergeants of The Queen's Own. The senior officers attended a reception at Government House in the evening.

The battalion's only internal security duty in May and June was to stand by while the Cypriots celebrated a Youth Festival on May 29. Town patrols continued during those two months in order to prevent clashes between provocative youths and the troops. For six weeks in July and August The Queen's Own were responsible for internal security in Nicosia. Tactical Headquarters were established in the main police station, and one company moved into the police station at Paphos Gate. Among the places guarded were an Ammunition Depot and Wayne's House, the residence of the Director of Operations. Although several large political rallies took place, there were no incidents which could not be dealt with by the civil police.

Lieutenant-Colonel D. H. Gwilliam, M.B.E., assumed command on July 28, on the departure of Lieutenant-Colonel A. J. M. Flint, M.B.E., to take up an appointment at Headquarters Allied Forces Central Europe. Colonel Flint sailed in the troopship "Dilwara" from Limassol on the 29th. Also on board was a Queen's Own advanced party, which was going to England to take over Moore Barracks at Shorncliffe, the battalion's next station.

Before Colonel Flint departed, he received a message from the Chief Constable of Cyprus. The message contained the following sentences: "I want to place on record the thanks of all ranks of the Cyprus Police Force for all the first-class work done by the battalion during the emergency. We have greatly admired your keenness and energy."

At the end of August, C.B.S. Camp was gradually demolished. Spare tents were taken down. The miniature range was dismantled. Tent boards, which were screening the messes and the offices, were removed. In the spaces thus laid bare rose piles of packing cases and stores in readiness for the move to England.

A farewell ceremonial parade took place on September 12. The battalion marched past in line and column of route. The salute was taken by the Director of Operations, who addressed the parade. In his speech Major-General Darling referred to the fine reputation gained by The Queen's Own in Cyprus, and wished good luck to all ranks on their return home. A further parade was held on the 17th for Brigadier Lister. This was a less formal affair, as the rifles had already been crated. The brigadier congratulated the troops on their high morale during their last few months on the island.

The battalion, less a rear-party, moved into Wayne's Keep Transit Camp on September 18. On the following day the rear-party struck C.B.S. Camp. During the ten days' stay at Wayne's Keep, inter-platoon football and basketball competitions were played. The band gave a farewell concert, which was recorded and later broadcast by the Cyprus Forces Broadcasting Service.

A fatigue party took the baggage by road to Limassol on the 26th. The main body followed on the 28th, and was taken out to the troopship "Devonshire" in small boats. Embarkation was accomplished in two hours. That evening Lieutenant-General Sir Roger Bower, C.-in-C. Middle East Land Forces, visited the ship to say goodbye. The families remained ashore in hotels for the night.

Early on September 29 His Excellency The Governor, Sir Hugh Foot, who had flown from Nicosia to Limasol by helicopter, went aboard to bid farewell. After talking to many of the troops, he breakfasted with the officers. As the "Devonshire" sailed at mid-day, the following message was received from Sir Hugh by Colonel Gwilliam:

> "I was very glad that I could visit you and your battalion in the "Devonshire" this morning to pay my respects to you and to express my gratitude to the battalion for all the fine work done in Cyprus over the past three years. The Royal West Kents have been in the thick of the troubles of the emergency and have answered every call made on them magnificently. They were in Cyprus long before I arrived, but I was particularly impressed by the most valuable contribution which they made in Nicosia during the bad days of last year. They were always ready to take action against violence and disorder in the capital and always available too for operations elsewhere. I am very happy that, before the battalion left, you could see better times on the island as we have been working out the settlement which the efforts of the Security Forces made possible. I very sincerely say thank you and good luck to you all."

So ended the last overseas tour and the last period of active service of the 1st Battalion The Queen's Own Royal West Kent Regiment (50th and 97th Foot).[1] Those Kentish Men and South Londoners had shown good humour in times of frustration, endurance during long days of fatigue, coolness in hours of excitement, and courage in moments of danger. They had done their duty well.

[1]For the story of the 1st Battalion from October 1959 to March 1961 see pages 63-66.

CHAPTER 5

Amalgamation

1. *The Amalgamation Parade*

AT 11 a.m. on March 1, 1961, a ceremony took place on the parade ground at Ross Barracks, Shorncliffe, to demonstrate the amalgamation of The Buffs (Royal East Kent Regiment) and The Queen's Own Royal West Kent Regiment, and, in particular, the merging of the 1st Battalions of the two regiments. On parade were two representative guards from the 1st Buffs under Lieutenant-Colonel Dendy, and two from the 1st Queen's Own under Lieutenant-Colonel Gwilliam. The Colours were carried by Lieutenants White and Cole (The Buffs) and Lieutenants Champion and Holman (The Queen's Own). As the Colonels of the two regiments stepped on to the dais, they were received with a General Salute. The two Colonels then inspected their respective guards. When the inspection was over, Lieutenant-Colonel Gwilliam marched off the ground; Lieutenant-Colonel Dendy assumed command of the four guards. The Colour Parties took post in the centre of the parade. Slowly, as the band played "Auld Lang Syne", the flags of The Buffs and The Queen's Own were lowered for the last time. To a fanfare of trumpets the flag of the new regiment was broken. The four guards, now representing the 1st Battalion of that regiment, marched past in slow time. Major-General Talbot delivered an address, during which he read messages from Her Majesty The Queen, His Majesty The King of Denmark, Her Royal Highness The Duchess of Kent and the

Lord Lieutenant of Kent. The ceremony ended with an advance in review order.

2. *Title and Colonels*

The Joint Amalgamation Committee, while resolving the problems which confronted it, had kept two main principles in mind. These were that all that was best in the traditions and history of The Buffs and The Queen's Own should be passed on to the new regiment; and that due weight should be given to the views of the serving personnel, as they would be responsible for forming and developing the new regiment.

The first problem had been to decide on the exact designation. It had been discussed by the past and present members of both regiments. There appeared to be two choices:—1, The main title should be The Royal Kent Regiment, with The Buffs and The Queen's Own in brackets. This was favoured by those who thought that the county connection was of primary importance. 2, The main title should be The Buffs and The Queen's Own, with The Royal Kent Regiment in brackets. Those who favoured this designation bore in mind the fact that The Buffs and, for a shorter period, The Queen's Own had long been famous names in the annals of the British Army. After the serving personnel of both regiments had again been consulted, the Joint Amalgamation Committee had formed the opinion that the designation should be " The Queen's Own Buffs, The Royal Kent Regiment," and that the short title should be " Queen's Own Buffs." This designation had been graciously approved by Her Majesty The Queen.

Her Majesty The Queen had also approved the following appointments:—His Majesty King Frederik IX of Denmark, who had been Colonel-in-Chief of The Buffs since 1947, to be Colonel-in-Chief; Her Royal Highness The Duchess of Kent to be Colonel of the Regiment; Major-General Talbot to be Deputy Colonel; and Major-General Craddock (lately The Buffs) to be Associate Colonel. Major-General Boucher (lately The Buffs) was to have been Deputy Colonel, but he was unable to take up the appointment because of ill-health; it is sad to relate that he died on April 1, 1961.

3. *Badge, Motto, Facings, Colours and Marches*

The Joint Amalgamation Committee had resolved that the regimental badge should be the White Horse of Kent with *Invicta*; that the motto should be *Veteri Frondescit Honore*, which had been used by The Buffs; that the facings and piping should be buff; and that the royal blue lanyard as worn by The Queen's Own should be retained. The regimental badge would be worn as a collar badge whenever appropriate.

The Regimental Colour was designed to commemorate The 3rd, The 50th and The 97th Foot. The Dragon (3rd) and the Lion and Crown (50th) were to be in opposite corners, and *Quo Fas et Gloria Ducunt* (97th) was to be below the badge and motto in the centre. The combined Battle Honours of The Buffs and The Queen's Own were to be emblazoned on the Colours, 35 being on The Queen's Colour and 39 on the Regimental. Of the total of 74 Battle Honours, 13 had been won by both regiments.

The regimental marches had been chosen with little difficulty. " The Men of Kent," which had been used by both regiments, was retained as the Slow March. A tune called " The Regimental Quick March of The Queen's Own Buffs, The Royal Kent Regiment," which was a combination of the best parts of " The Buffs " and "A Hundred Pipers," was adopted as the Quick March; it had been composed by Mr. Lynes, the bandmaster of The Buffs. Similarly, a combination of the bugle calls of both regiments was adopted as the Regimental Bugle Call.

4. *Headquarters, the Regimental Association and Journal*

The original intention had been that the Regimental Headquarters should be at Maidstone. But when the plans had been studied, it had been found that the proposed building would be unsuitable. So, since adequate accommodation had been available at Canterbury and the Home Counties Brigade Depot was located there, it had been decided that the main headquarters should be established at Canterbury, leaving an "increment" at Maidstone to maintain the link with the County Town. This "increment," with Lieut-Colonel Eason in charge, was temporarily accommodated in the old Mobilisation Block in the barracks at Maidstone. Colonel Eason was later relieved by Lieutenant-Colonel Grove.

The Past and Present Associations of both regiments amalgamated to form " The Regimental Association of The Queen's Own Buffs, The Royal Kent Regiment." The first Chairman was Lieutenant-Colonel Edwards, with Lieutenant-Colonel Argles (lately The Buffs) as Vice-Chairman. All branches of The Queen's Own Past and Present Association joined the new association, and all Service Battalion branches became affiliated to it. In London, where each regiment had a numerically strong branch, the two branches continued to hold separate meetings. The Shorncliffe Branch of The Queen's Own merged with the Folkestone Branch of The Buffs to form the Folkestone, Hythe and District Branch.

The Queen's Own Gazette was published for the last time in February 1961. The first issue of *Invicta*, the regimental journal of The Queen's Own Buffs, appeared in the following month. It was printed by the *Kent Messenger* and was edited by Colonel Grace (lately The Buffs). It contained all the features which had been familiar to readers of The Q.O.G.

5. *Customs and Memorials*

The customs of both regiments were handed on to The Queen's Own Buffs, The Royal Kent Regiment. Those concerning The Queen's Own were:—

1. Piping Dinners. This custom and the one which follows were links with the period in 1778 when The 50th Foot fought as marines at the naval battle off Ushant.
2. Playing " Rule Britannia " before the regimental marches on Guest Nights in the officers' mess.

3. Laying a wreath at the foot of Nelson's Column on Trafalgar Day to commemorate the period in 1794 when The 50th served with Nelson in Corsica.
4. Toasting " The Corunna Majors " on January 16 to commemorate Majors Napier and Stanhope, who led the counter-attack of The 50th at the Battle of Corunna in 1809.
5. Turning a page of each Book of Remembrance in All Saints' Church, Maidstone, each week. After amalgamation, this was done by a member of the Maidstone Company of the 4th/5th Battalion.
6. Observing September 8 (Sevastopol Day) as a Regimental Day. The Buffs' Day—May 16 (Albuhera Day)—was also retained as a Regimental Day.
7. Inviting the officers of The King's Own Scottish Borderers to consider themselves permanent honorary members of the officers' mess of the 1st Battalion, in memory of the close comradeship which had existed between the 1st Battalion The Queen's Own and the 2nd Battalion The King's Own Scottish Borderers during the 1914-1918 War. (See *The Queen's Own Royal West Kent Regiment, 1920-1950,* page 55.)

The responsibility for the maintenance of the Memorials to the dead of both regiments was assumed by The Queen's Own Buffs. Details of the Memorials to The Queen's Own can be found in Appendix F.

6. *Freedoms and Alliances*

The Borough Council of Maidstone resolved that the Honorary Freedom of the Borough, which had been granted to The Queen's Own in 1944, should be extended to The Queen's Own Buffs, The Royal Kent Regiment. Similarly, the Town Councils of Canterbury and Ramsgate decided that the Honorary Freedoms of their Towns, which had been bestowed on The Buffs, should be carried forward to the new regiment. The Freedom of Folkestone was conferred on The Queen's Own Buffs, and the Urban District Council of Tonbridge formally adopted the regiment.

PRIVATE R. LUTHER, 4TH/5TH BATTALION, TURNING A PAGE OF A QUEEN'S OWN BOOK OF REMEMBRANCE IN ALL SAINTS' CHURCH, 6TH NOVEMBER, 1961.

The alliances with the following regiments of the Dominions were transferred to The Queen's Own Buffs:—

From The Queen's Own—The Canterbury Regiment (New Zealand)
The Royal New Brunswick Regiment (Canada)
The Essex and Kent Scottish (Canada).

From The Buffs— The Queen's Own Rifles of Canada

7. *Silver, Property and Finance*

Boards had been convened in the 1st Battalion The Queen's Own and at the Depot to check all silver and property and to recommend how it should be distributed. A considerable quantity of the silver and property was passed on to the 1st Battalion The Queen's Own Buffs. Some of the articles not required by that unit were sent " on long loan " to the Home Counties Brigade Depot and to the 4th/5th Battalion. Others were loaned to Schools of Instruction, Staff Colleges, Corps messes, Cadet units, etc. The remainder were offered for sale to retired and serving personnel of the regiment.

A Joint Financial Committee had been convened. It had resolved that, in general, the funds of the two regiments should be amalgamated. The main exceptions concerning The Queen's Own were:—

The Compassionate Fund and Leckie Bequest, which remained a Trust Fund to assist past and present members of The Queen's Own.

The Fitton Benefaction, which remained a Trust Fund to assist widows of officers of The Queen's Own.

The Queen's Own Gazette Fund. A grant of £500 was made to the Regimental Journal Fund of The Queen's Own Buffs; the balance was transferred to The Queen's Own Museum Fund.

The Relics Fund, which remained part of The Queen's Own Museum Fund.

The Grove Trust, which was transferred to the 1st Battalion The Queen's Own Buffs.

8. *Social and Sporting Functions*

The problems concerning the social and sporting functions of The Queen's Own Buffs, The Royal Kent Regiment had been resolved as follows:—The Annual Re-unions at both Canterbury and Maidstone should continue; the Officers' Dinner Clubs of The Buffs and The Queen"s Own should amalgamate to form the Regimental Dinner Club of The Queen's Own Buffs; the Colours for Games should be buff and royal blue (the colours of the facings of The Buffs and The Queen's Own); the Regimental Tie should be buff and royal blue, either in broad stripes or, alternatively, in narrow buff stripes on a royal blue background; Regimental Tents should be erected at both the Canterbury and the Maidstone Cricket Weeks; and the Golfing Societies of The Buffs and The Queen's Own should amalgamate to form The Queen's Own Buffs Golfing Society.

9. *Conclusion*

The Queen's Own Royal West Kent Regiment has ceased to exist as a separate regiment. But, from the details given in this chapter, there is every reason to believe that by its fusion with The Buffs (Royal East Kent Regiment) there has come forth a regiment which will maintain and cherish its customs and traditions. This belief was aptly expressed by the Colonel of the Regiment in his reply to the Mayor of Maidstone's address on the occasion of the Farewell Parade of the Depot on February 28, 1961. General Talbot said:—" The Queen's Own Buffs, The Royal Kent Regiment, which comes into being tomorrow, will not be a new regiment. It will be a continuation of two very old and distinguished regiments with long histories and great traditions. Moreover, as a result of this amalgamation, a truly County regiment will emerge . . . "

Roll of Honour

1946-1961

A List of Members of THE QUEEN'S OWN who lost their lives on active service.

IN MALAYA

	Gibson, J. M., Captain	13.11.1949	Killed

IN KOREA

14189156	Page, D. O., Private	27.10.1950	Of wounds

IN KENYA

5780141	Horswell, A. W. Col.-Sgt.	18. 8.1953	Accidentally shot

WITH THE 1st BATTALION IN MALAYA

22408075	Coleman, D. C., Private[1]	10.10.1951	Disease
	Deed, E. A., Captain	22.10.1951	Killed
22787516	Denton, C., Private[1]	11. 9.1952	Killed
6343399	Henderson, T. H., Corporal	30. 9.1951	Of wounds
22413906	Hollebon, L. G., Private[1]	22. 8.1951	Of wounds
22466887	Latter, D. W., Private[1]	6.11.1952	Killed
22442053	Lepper, A. G., Private[1]	24.10.1951	Of wounds
22455961	Lowday, W. J., Private[1]	10. 4.1952	Killed
	Manning, D. W., 2nd Lieut.[1]	23. 4.1953	Killed
6343275	Newell, E. C., Lance-Cpl.	22. 2.1954	Disease

[1]National Service.

WITH THE 1st BATTALION IN CYPRUS

23012468	Martin, R. S. J., Private[1]	3. 3.1957	Accidentally shot

Members of OTHER REGIMENTS who lost their lives on active service with the 1st Battalion

IN MALAYA

22439555	Bardell, J., Pte.[1]	22.10.51	Killed	E. Surrey
22442015	Brown D., Pte.[1]	22.10.51	Killed	E. Surrey
22126648	Chambers, R. J., L/C.	22.10.51	Killed	E. Surrey
22418822	Cheeseman, J., Pte.[1]	22.10.51	Killed	E. Surrey
22442030	Elsley, D. R. I., Pte.[1]	6. 9.51	Killed	E. Surrey
22308280	Hand, L. J., Pte.	22.10.51	Killed	Buffs
6142255	Heath, G., Pte.	22.10.51	Killed	E. Surrey
22309796	Holman, L., Pte.	26.11.51	Killed	E. Surrey
22397095	Knight, J. A. C., Pte.[1]	22.10.51	Killed	R. Fusiliers
21070715	Molland, D. P., L/C.	22.10.51	Killed	R. Fusiliers
22382276	Pelling, M. H., Pte.[1]	22.10.51	Killed	R. Sussex
22259843	Stevenson, H. G., Pte.	1. 7.53	Accident	E. Surrey
14471068	Sulley, H., Cpl.	22.10.51	Killed	R. Fusiliers
22541537	Villers, R. E., Pte.	13.11.52	Disease	R. Fusiliers
22309399	Whitmore, P. A., Pte.	4. 1.52	Traffic Accident	R. Sussex

IN CYPRUS

6090692	O'Gorman, J. J., Cpl.	6. 7.57	Traffic Accident	Queen's

IBAN TRACKERS who lost their lives on active service with the 1st Battalion IN MALAYA

Bulang, Private	22.10.51	Killed.
Kelambu, Private	22.10.51	Killed.
Untang, Private	22.10.51	Killed.

[1] National Service.

Bibliography

J. MacCarthy, late 50th Regiment. "Recollections of the Storming of Badajos." Published in 1836.

Major J. Patterson. "Adventures of Captain John Patterson, with Notices of the officers of The 50th Regiment, 1807-21."

Major J. Patterson. "Camp and Quarters. Scenes and Impressions of Military Life." Two volumes. Published in 1840.

Catherine M. Marsh. "Memorials of Captain Hedley Vicars, 97th Regiment." Published in 1856.

Lieutenant-General Sir William Napier. "The Life and Opinions of General Sir Charles James Napier." Biographies of this distinguished 50th officer were also written by W. N. Bruce and General Sir William Butler.

Thomas McKiernan. "Experiences of a British Veteran Soldier." The author was a Colour-Sergeant in The 50th Regiment.

"The Queen's Own Gazette." Published monthly from 1875 to 1961.

"The Queen's Own Almanack." Published from 1892 to 1895. Copies are in the British Museum Library.

Colonel A. E. Fyler. "The History of The 50th or (The Queen's Own) Regiment."

Anonymous. Articles in "Navy and Army Illustrated." 11th March and 5th August 1899.

John Stirling. Chapter on the 2nd Battalion in "Our Regiments in South Africa, 1899-1902."

R. de M. Rudolf. Pamphlet outlining the Regiment's Services. Published by H.M.S.O. in 1905.

Walter Wood (as told to). Chapter in "Survivors Tales of Great Events." Relating to Sikh War experiences.

Colonel J. Bonhote. "Historical Records of the West Kent Militia." Published for private circulation in 1909.

Lieutenant-Colonel J. J. Anderson. "Recollections of a Peninsular Veteran." Published in 1913.

H. J. Wenyon and H. S. Brown. "The History of the 8th Battalion The Queen's Own Royal West Kent Regiment, 1914-1919." Published for private circulation in 1921.

Major C. V. Molony. "Invicta." With the 1st Battalion The Queen's Own Royal West Kent Regiment in the Great War."

C. T. Atkinson. "The Queen's Own Royal West Kent Regiment, 1914-1919."

Lieutenant H. N. Edwards, Medal Roll. Part 1, 1793-1881, was published in 1928. Part 2, 1882-1902, was published in "The Queen's Own Gazette," January-December 1933.

Anonymous. "A Short History of The Queen's Own Royal West Kent Regiment." Printed by the Kent Messenger in 1930.

Captain H. N. Edwards. "A Short Record of the Colours of The Queen's Own Royal West Kent Regiment." Reprinted from "The Queen's Own Gazette" in 1933.

Captain R. O. Russell. "History of the 11th (Lewisham) Battalion The Queen's Own Royal West Kent Regiment, 1914-1918." Published in 1934.

Captain H. N. Edwards. Articles on "The Clothing, Equipment and Arms of The Queen's Own, 1756-1936." Printed in "The Queen's Own Gazette" in 1937-1938.

Michael Joseph. "The Sword in the Scabbard." The author served in the 9th Battalion in 1940-1941.

Lieutenant-Colonel H. D. Chaplin. "The Queen's Own Royal West Kent Regiment, 1920-1950."

Lieutenant-Colonel H. D. Chaplin. "The Queen's Own Royal West Kent Regiment. A Short Account of its Origins, Service and Campaigns, 1756-1956."

Lieutenant-Colonel H. D. Chaplin. "The Queen's Own Royal West Kent Regiment, 1881-1914." Published in 1959.

Walter Robson. "Letters from a Soldier." The author was a Lance-Corporal serving with the 1st Battalion in North Africa, Italy and Greece, 1943-1945. Published by Faber and Faber in 1960.

Christopher Hibbert. "Corunna." An account of the retreat to and action at Corunna, in which The 50th took a prominent part. Published by B. T. Batsford Ltd. in 1961.

Majors E. B. S. Clarke and A. T. Tillott. "From Kent to Kohima". With the 4th Battalion (T.A.), 1939-1947.

Appendices

APPENDIX A

Roll of Colonels and Commanding Officers

1951-1961

Colonel-in-Chief

H.R.H. The Duchess of Kent, C.I., G.C.V.O., G.B.E. May 12, 1947.

Colonels of the Regiment

Lieut.-Gen. Sir William P. Oliver, K.C.B., O.B.E., D.L. Jan. 17, 1949.
Major-Gen. D. E. B. Talbot, C.B., C.B.E., D.S.O., M.C. Oct. 15 1959.

Regimental Depot

Major	C. H. Keenlyside	7. 7.48—31. 3.52
Major	R. E. Moss	1. 4.52—19. 5.55
Major	H. B. H. Waring	20. 5.55—21. 6.57
Major	G. U. Weymouth, M.B.E.	22. 6.57—20. 1.60
Major	I. A. Macmillan	21. 1.60—27.12.60
Major	J. D. Norton	28.12.60—31. 3.61

Closed.

1st Battalion (50th and 97th)

Lieut.-Col.	A. Martyn, O.B.E.	8.10.48—19. 1.52
Lieut.-Col.	G. G. Elliott, D.S.O.	20. 1.52—16.12.52
Major	P. C. M. Buckle (Acting)	17.12.52— 8. 3.53
Lieut.-Col.	A. R. Fyler, O.B.E.	9. 3.53—13. 2.55
Major	A. J. M. Flint, M.B.E. (Acting)	14. 2.55—12. 3.55
Lieut.-Col.	P. C. M. Buckle	13. 3.55— 8. 2.57
Major	A. J. M. Flint, M.B.E. (Acting)	9. 2.57—30. 3.57
Lieut.-Col.	A. J. M. Flint, M.B.E.	31. 3.57—27. 7.59
Lieut.-Col.	D. H. Gwilliam, M.B.E.	28. 7.59—28. 2.61

Amalgamated with the 1st Battalion The Buffs (Royal East Kent Regiment) as the 1st Battalion The Queen's Own Buffs, The Royal Kent Regiment.

4th/5th Battalion

Honorary Colonels

Colonel	W. Nash, M.B.E., T.D.	Sep. 25. 1947
Brigadier	H. S. Brown, M.C., T.D.	Sep. 25. 1953
Lieut.-Col.	G. E. L. Pardington, M.B.E., T.D.	Sep. 25. 1958

Commanding Officers

Lieut.-Col.	C. A. de B. Brounlie, M.C.	9. 6.48— 9. 5.51
Lieut.-Col.	L. F. W. Jackson	10. 5.51— 8. 5.54
Lieut.-Col.	C. H. Keenlyside	9. 5.54— 7. 5.57
Lieut.-Col.	A. R. H. Waring, T.D.	8. 5.57—30. 9.60
Lieut.-Col.	T. C. Coath, T.D.	1.10.60—

APPENDIX B

Honours and Awards

Part 1 — 1920 - 1939

THE ORDER OF THE BATH

Knight Commander

Bonham-Carter, C., C.B., C.M.G., D.S.O., Lieutenant-General, Jan. 1935
Hildyard, R. J. T., C.B., C.M.G., D.S.O., Lieutenant-General, Jan. 1936
O'Dowda, J. W., C.B., C.S.I., C.M.G., Lieutenant-General, Jan. 1934

Companion

Bonham-Carter, C., C.M.G., D.S.O., Major-General, June 1926
Hildyard, R. J. T., C. M. G., D.S.O., Brigadier, June 1928
Isacke, H., C.S.I., C.M.G., Colonel, Jan. 1922.
Martyn, A. Wood, D.S.O., O.B.E., Colonel, June 1930

THE ORDER OF THE BRITISH EMPIRE

(Military Division)

Officer

Grey, F., D.C.M., Lieutenant-Colonel (Quartermaster), June 1930

Member

Wilkin, H., M.C., Captain, June 1923

(Civil Division)

Officer

Clay, B. L., Captain, June 1933

THE MILITARY CROSS

Fry, O. M., Captain, Oct. 1925 (Kurdistan 1924)

THE BRITISH EMPIRE MEDAL

McEwen, S., W.O.1 (Bandmaster), Jan. 1934 (Seconded to The R.W.A.F.F.)

EGYPTIAN ORDER OF THE NILE, THIRD CLASS

Brock, R. G. C., O.B.E., Major, March 1931

WITH THE SECOND BATTALION IN PALESTINE, 1938-1939

THE DISTINGUISHED SERVICE ORDER

Bryan, D. C. S., Major

THE ORDER OF THE BRITISH EMPIRE

Officer

Travers, R. L., Major

THE MILITARY CROSS

Grove, M. R. L., 2nd Lieutenant
Read, M. R., Lieutenant
Rooke, D. B., 2nd Lieutenant
Whitty, J. H. H., Lieutenant

THE MILITARY MEDAL

Richards, F. C., Private
Sparkes, L. E., Private

Part 2 — 1951 - 1961

THE ORDER OF THE BATH

Knight Commander

Oliver, W. P., C.B., O.B.E., Lieutenant-General, May 1956

Companion

Rome, F. D., C.B.E., D.S.O., Major-General, Jan. 1955
Talbot,, D. E. B., C.B.E., D.S.O., M.C., Major-General, Jan. 1960
Tarver, C. H., C.B.E., D.S.O., Major-General, Jan. 1961.

THE ORDER OF THE BRITISH EMPIRE

(Military Division)

Commander

Chitty, A. A. E., D.S.O., Colonel, June 1955
Talbot, D. E. B., D.S.O., M.C., Brigadier, May 1955 (Malaya)
Tarver, C. H., D.S.O., Major-General, June 1958

Officer

Bernard, C. M., Lieutenant-Colonel, June 1959
Jackson, D. W., Brevet-Lieutenant-Colonel, June 1954
Martyn, A., Lieutenant-Colonel, June 1951

Member

Cook. E. S., Captain (Quartermaster), Jan. 1955
Grubb, J. E., W.O.II (R.Q.M.S.), May 1956
Gwilliam, D. H., Major, June 1954 (Malaya, Staff)
Morris, D., W.O.I (R.S.M.), June 1953
Nicholls, R. W. G., Captain, Oct. 1953 (Malaya, Staff)
Stock, P. R., Captain, June 1958 (Malaya, with The R. Malay Regt.)
Theobald, F. K., T.D., Major, May 1956
Willis, C. F., T.D., Major, Jan. 1955

(Civil Division)

Member

Peploe, H., D.S.O., Colonel (Retd.), Jan. 1955.
Snoad, H. G. C., ex-WO.II (C.S.M.), Jan. 1961.

THE BRITISH EMPIRE MEDAL

Marshall, L., Colour-Sergeant, Jan. 1955
Selmes, A. G., W.O.II (R.Q.M.S.), Jan. 1961

U.S.A. BRONZE STAR MEDAL

Thomas, R. C. W, Major, Oct. 1953 (Korea, Staff).

AHLI MANGKO NEGARA (MALAYAN PANUKA ORDER)

Woodmar, E. G., M.C., Major, June 1959

BREVET PROMOTIONS

Crook, P. E., O.B.E., Major to Brevet-Lieut.-Col., July 1953
Gwilliam, D. H., M.B.E., Major to Brevet-Lieut.-Col., July 1958
Jackson, D. W., Major to Brevet-Lieut.-Col., July 1953
Manners, D. C. J., Major to Brevet-Lieut.-Col., July 1956

MENTIONED IN DESPATCHES

Abplanalp, V. C., Captain, 1956 (Kenya, Staff)
Barrett, A. L., W.O.II, 1954 (Malaya)
Bryant, A. E., Sergeant, 1952 (Malaya)
Maclachlan, S., 2nd Lieutenant, 1955 (Kenya)
Martyn, A., O.B.E., Lieutenant-Colonel, 1953 (Malaya, Staff)
Read, M. R., M.C., Lieutenant-Colonel, 1959 (Arabia)
Thomas, R. C. W., Major, 1952 (Korea, Staff)
Watts, R. A., 2nd Lieutenant, 1954 (Malaya)

COMMANDER-IN-CHIEF'S COMMENDATION CARD

Garrett, N., Sergeant, 1953 (Korea)

WITH THE FIRST BATTALION IN MALAYA, 1951-1954

THE ORDER OF THE BRITISH EMPIRE

Officer

Fyler, A. R., Lieutenant-Colonel

Member

Sivers, A. E., M.M., Major (Quartermaster)
Upton, T. V., Major
Watkins, R. G., W.O.I (Bandmaster)

THE MILITARY CROSS

Beale, K. S., Lieutenant
Howlett, G. H. W., 2nd Lieutenant
Leigh, P. S., Lieutenant
Neve, R. W., 2nd Lieutenant

THE DISTINGUISHED CONDUCT MEDAL

Gordon, G. R., Sergeant
Pannell, J. L., Private

THE MILITARY MEDAL

Clark, D. F., Corporal (Middlesex Regiment)
Healey, R. V. C., Sergeant
Martin, J. C., Lance-Corporal
Wilde, K. J., Sergeant
Sanggau, Private (Iban Tracker)

THE BRITISH EMPIRE MEDAL

Dallen, A., W.O.II (C.S.M.)
King, H. J., Sergeant
Watts, G. V. K., W.O.II (C.S.M.)

MENTIONED IN DESPATCHES

Ball, B. D., Corporal
Beale, K. S., Lieutenant
Buckle, P. C. M., Major
Butcher, J., Drummer
Campbell, D. P. I., Captain
Chitty, G. A. J., Corporal
Crook, P. E., O.B.E., Major
Dodson, K., Captain
Dover, V., M.C., Major
Flint, A. J. M., M.B.E., Major
Follett-Smith, F. A., 2nd Lieutenant
Fyler, A. R., Lieutenant-Colonel
Gordon, G. R., Sergeant
Grubb, J. E., W.O.II (R.Q.M.S.)
Haley, A., Corporal
Healey, R. V. C., Corporal
King, H. J., Sergeant
Leigh, P. S., Lieutenant
Lemar, R. D., Sergeant (Royal Fusiliers)
Levett, G. E., Sergeant (The Buffs)
Manktelow, D. W., Lance-Corporal
Neve, R. W., 2nd Lieutenant
Newall, M. R. M., 2nd Lieutenant
Parish, J., Lance-Corporal
Payne, J. F. E., Private
Proctor, H., Sergeant
Quinn, E., Sergeant
Roper, I. H., M.C., Major
Singleton, J., Lance-Corporal
Smith, G. H. S., Sergeant (Queen's Royal Regiment)
Stock, P. R., Lieutenant
Waring, H. B. H., Major
Wilson, J. B., Captain
Wilson, R. D. H., 2nd Lieutenant
Woolstencroft, D. H., Lieutenant

COMMANDER-IN-CHIEF'S CERTIFICATE

Batchelor, R., Lance-Corporal
McCracken, R. H. W., Band-Sergeant
Martin, B. L., Sergeant
Parker, A. G., Sergeant
Smith, D. N., Private
Thornton, J., W.O.II (C.S.M.)
Vine, R. W., Sergeant
Wheeler, A. E., Private

ROYAL HUMANE SOCIETY BRONZE MEDAL

Searles, F., Private

THE SUEZ INTERVENTION, 1956

THE DISTINGUISHED SERVICE ORDER

Crook, P. E., O.B.E., Lieutenant-Colonel (Comd. 3rd Bn. Parachute Regt.)

MENTIONED IN DESPATCHES

Dowse, R. K., Major (With the 1st Battalion)
Newall, M. R. M., Lieutenant (Attached 3rd Bn. Parachute Regt.)
Osborne, E. C. S., Captain (With the 1st Battalion)

WITH THE FIRST BATTALION IN CYPRUS, 1956-1959

THE ORDER OF THE BRITISH EMPIRE

Member

Parker, A. G., W.O.I (R.S.M.)
Simpson, G. V. I., W.O.II (R.Q.M.S.)
Waring, H. B. H., Major

MENTIONED IN DESPATCHES

Champion, C. G., 2nd Lieutenant
Dodson, K., Captain
Flint, A. J. M., M.B.E., Lieutenant-Colonel
Locker, T. J. B., 2nd Lieutenant

COMMANDER-IN-CHIEF'S CERTIFICATE

Brown, G., Sergeant
Levett, G. E., Colour-Sergeant
Skelding, D., Sergeant
Woolgar, N., Sergeant

Part 3 — Citations for Gallantry (Malaya)

THE MILITARY CROSS

Lieutenant K. S. Beale.—Lieutenant Beale arrived in Malaya with the battalion two-and-a-half years ago and, except for a short period when he carried out the duties of Intelligence Officer, he has been in command of an operational platoon the entire time. He has led many patrols and ambushes, during which his platoon has accounted for seven terrorists, of which he personally killed three.

In December 1952 he located a small Communist terrorist camp on the Ulu Caledonia Estate. He had only six men with him. With five of these he formed a stop party, whilst he proceeded to stalk the terrorist sentry with his Bren gunner. He managed to get within 15 yards of the sentry when he was forced to open fire. He killed the sentry.

In February 1953 Lieutenant Beale was leading a small patrol on the Mantatt Estate when he was fired on by three terrorists at very close range. He at once returned the fire and wounded one terrorist, the others taking to flight. The wounded terrorist threw a grenade, which landed a yard from him and fortunately failed to explode. Without hesitation he charged up the slope, killed the terrorist and then organised the follow-up of the remaining terrorists.

The following day he led a further patrol into the same estate and himself killed another terrorist.

It was his platoon, led by him, which opened the battalion's score one day after its arrival in the operational area in March 1951.

Lieutenant Beale is an inspired leader of men, of dauntless courage and determination. He has shown quite exceptional powers of leadership, bravery and endurance over a very long period.

2nd Lieutenant G. H. W. Howlett.—On February 21, 1952, 2nd Lieutenant Howlett led out his platoon to find and destroy a bandit camp in the Beruntang area, Ulu Selangor. The approach necessitated a 36-hours patrol through varied and difficult country. By skilful navigation the bandit camp was found in the jungle and attacked by 2nd Lieutenant Howlett. It was, however, found to be empty, having been only recently vacated. Useful documents were found in the camp, and the body of a bandit, who had been executed, was discovered.

2nd Lieutenant Howlett wisely avoided returning by the same route. As the leading scout emerged from the edge of the jungle on an oil palm estate, he saw five bandits at about 100 yards range. 2nd Lieutenant Howlett made a quick plan. He sent one section round on a flank on high ground to cut off the bandits, and ordered his platoon sergeant to give covering fire with the platoon headquarters group. He himself led the second section in a direct attack on the enemy. The bandits returned heavy fire and then, alternately moving and firing, tried to escape. 2nd Lieutenant Howlett led his men in hot pursuit over hilly country, in which good cover was plentiful. With dash and determination all five bandits were closely engaged and, after spirited encounters over a period of some 20 minutes, during which time the bandits continued to resist bravely, all were eventually killed. 2nd Lieutenant Howlett, at the head of his men, personally accounted for two of them. There were no casualties to our troops.

2nd Lieutenant Howlett's mastery of jungle conditions, his rapid thinking, sensible plan and courageous leadership were outstanding throughout and were the main reason for the complete success of the action. The bandits killed proved to be members of an M.R.L.A. platoon, which had previously taken part in major offensive actions against the Security Forces. 2nd Lieutenant Howlett's personal example in leading the attack on these bandits with no regard for his personal safety resulted in the elimination of an entire group of a strong bandit platoon, which will have an adverse effect on the future morale of the enemy in this area.

This was no isolated incident. On the night before this patrol, 2nd Lieutenant Howlett was in command of an ambush party which killed one bandit and wounded another. This success was due entirely to 2nd Lieutenant Howlett's excellent positioning of the ambush, quick thinking and personal example.

These successful actions complete a year of outstanding work by 2nd Lieutenant Howlett on operations, during which time he has been personally responsible for the killing of eight bandits. Throughout, he has maintained a consistently high standard of good example and leadership.

Lieutenant P. S. Leigh.—Lieutenant Leigh arrived in Malaya with the battalion nearly three years ago and has served with it the whole time. He commanded an operational platoon for two years and subsequently took over the duties of Intelligence Officer.

As a rifle platoon commander he made a name for himself as a particularly courageous and skilful leader. In May 1951, on Ulu Selangor Estate, his platoon ambushed and killed three Communist terrorists, one of whom was a State committee member and one the quartermaster for North Selangor. The success of this ambush was entirely due to Lieutenant Leigh's skilful placing of the position. He himself fired the first shot and killed the first bandit. In July 1952 he was in command of his platoon when it killed a Communist terrorist on Sungei Gumut Estate.

As Battalion Intelligence Officer, Lieutenant Leigh continued to show a high standard of efficiency. His new duties did not prevent him from taking every opportunity of going out against the terrorists with other companies and platoons, such was his enthusiasm for active operations.

In June 1953 he joined a Special Branch police force in a dawn raid on a squatter area in the Cheras Road district of Kuala Lumpur. An unknown number of bandits was located in a hidden department at water level in a well. Two bandits, having shouted that they would surrender, treacherously threw two grenades one after the other out of the well. One grenade landed two yards and the other three yards away from Lieutenant Leigh. The two bandits leapt out of the well. One escaped through the cordon of Security Forces as the first grenade detonated. The other came straight at Lieutenant Leigh, who, quite regardless of his own safety in that the second grenade was three yards away from him and apparently about to go off, rose to his feet and riddled the terrorist with bullets. Fortunately, the grenade failed to explode. Lieutenant Leigh then took a leading part in capturing four other bandits in the area, making a total of five eliminations in one action in which his personal example was quite outstanding for courage, skill and determination.

In September 1953, while still carrying out the duties of Battalion Intelligence Officer, Lieutenant Leigh was in command of one group of a specially-picked night ambush party, which killed two Communist couriers as they were running along a track in the Serendah Forest.

In three days this same operational party, in which he commanded a group, accounted for a total of six terrorists.

Lieutenant Leigh has been in numerous operations during the past three years, and in all of them he has shown the very highest qualities of courage, leadership and determination. The successful actions which he has fought over a long period have been the greatest inspiration to the whole battalion.

2nd Lieutenant R. W. Neve.—During the whole time he has been in Malaya—more than 18 months—2nd Lieutenant Neve has been in command of an operational platoon, which he has led in many ambushes and patrols. Between September 1953 and February 1954 his platoon and other small forces, all but one under his command, have contacted 11 terrorists, killing no fewer than 10, of whom he himself killed two.

In September 1953 he led a small assault group on a camp occupied by four terrorists. The track used by the assault group was only two feet wide, but 2nd Lieutenant Neve led the way and, although fired on at short range, he charged the camp with such determination that all four terrorists were killed. One of the terrorists killed was a branch committee member wanted for murder.

In November and December 1953 he commanded assault groups which killed three terrorists out of four contacted.

In January 1954, while commanding two platoons, he discovered an occupied terrorist camp. He detailed the majority of his force to encircle the camp, while he led a small assault group close up to it. But the sentry saw them and opened fire. Immediately, 2nd Lieutenant Neve charged the camp, going so fast that he out-distanced his assault group and arrived in the camp on his own, where he shot two terrorists dead.

He has shown outstanding qualities of courage, determination and endurance over a long period. His invariable personal and successful leadership of his assault groups and his utter disregard for danger have been the greatest inspiration to his platoon and the whole battalion.

THE DISTINGUISHED CONDUCT MEDAL

Sergeant G. R. Gordon.—Sergeant Gordon arrived with the battalion in Malaya nearly three years ago and has taken part in operations the whole time. He has personally killed at least two terrorists and has been in ambushes and other actions that have accounted for 11 terrorist eliminations.

In February 1952, on the Leonardo Estate, the patrol which he was commanding was attacked by terrorists, who were armed with light machine guns. He organised a counter-attack and rapidly put the enemy to flight, only darkness and heavy rain impeding pursuit.

In the same month he was commanding his section in an ambush on Behrang Estate, when two terrorists entered the ambush. Both were killed by the section's fire, personally directed by him.

In April 1953 he commanded a group in an ambush on the Waverley Estate. Two terrorists, both branch committee members, entered the ambush and both were killed, one by him personally.

In July 1953 he commanded a section of the Assault Pioneer Platoon in an ambush on the Kerling Kechil river track. One terrorist, a branch committee member with a considerable reputation in the neighbourhood, approached the ambush position alone, but, sensing the presence of Security Forces, started to draw a grenade from his belt. Before he could pull out the pin, Sergeant Gordon shot him dead.

In September 1953 he was a member of a specially-picked night ambush party which killed two Communist couriers as they were running along a track in the Serendah Forest. In three days the same operational party, in which he commanded a group, accounted for a total of six terrorists.

In nearly three years of continuous operations he has acquired a reputation for fearlessness, resource and aggression that has spread through the whole of North Selangor. He has been an automatic choice for any special operational party which has been formed. His enthusiasm, leadership and drive over a very long period have been outstanding.

Private J. L. Pannell.—This senior Regular private soldier was a member of the escort which took out three vehicles to collect a platoon of his company which had completed an operational patrol. On the return journey on October 22, 1951, after picking up the platoon, Private Pannell was travelling in the leading unarmoured three-ton lorry through the Ulu Caledonia Estate, North Selangor. The convoy was ambushed in a defile by a highly-organised and well-led gang of at least 30 bandits armed with automatic weapons, rifles and grenades. His vehicle bore the brunt of the first intense fire that was opened on the convoy. The senior officer and platoon sergeant were killed instantly, and the other officer was severely wounded. Before firing had gone on for long, only 16 men of the whole convoy remained alive, and of these all but three were wounded, some more than once and others very badly.

At first, Private Pannell gave whole-hearted and courageous support to the young lance-corporal who alone remained effective from the officers in his vehicle, and, when this N.C.O. was hit, took command of the situation himself. By the personal example of moving about without regard to danger, by the shouting of encouragement and sharp orders, and by the effective use of grenades and his personal weapon, Private Pannell inspired his comrades to fight back with everything they had. Further, by astute battle appreciation of the enemy's intentions, he so applied his own and his comrades' fire as to halt at least two hostile rushes and, generally, to break the enemy's will to continue the fight.

It was largely due to his courage and leadership that, after about an hour's fighting, the enemy withdrew, leaving six of their dead and three of their weapons, and with their object of capturing the platoon's arms completely frustrated. By the end, Private Pannell had been hit four times, but, after giving what aid he could to the other wounded, he set off with one other man to walk two miles through dangerous country to obtain help.

THE MILITARY MEDAL

Corporal D. F. Clark (The Middlesex Regiment).—In March 1953 Corporal Clark was commanding his sub-section in an operation on the Belata River Rubber Estate. While resting at a rendezvous on a track, several Communist terrorists approached the position. He allowed the terrorists to come on until their leading scout was only 15 yards away. He then shot him dead. The following terrorists immediately opened fire, including automatic weapons, at this N.C.O. and his sub-section. Showing great coolness and complete disregard for his personal safety, he directed the fire of his group to such effect that the enemy withdrew. At least one terrorist was severely wounded.

He then led his sub-section in immediate pursuit, but failed to make further contact.

This N.C.O. came out with the battalion two-and-a-half years ago. He has taken part in many anti-bandit actions, in all of which he has shown coolness and determination. He has on every occasion when action was joined displayed inspired and confident leadership with no regard whatsoever to personal safety.

Sergeant R. V. C. Healey.—Sergeant Healey arrived with the battalion in Malaya nearly three years ago. He has taken part in numerous patrols and ambushes and has at least two bandits to his personal credit.

On October 4, 1951, Sergeant Healey, then a lance-corporal in command of his section, contacted three terrorists in the Kerling area and killed one personally, one other being wounded.

In January 1952, with eight men of his platoon, he was in an ambush position on the Leonardo Estate when 12 terrorists came towards him in two parties from different directions. During the confused action which resulted, he so controlled the battle and inspired the men under his command that three terrorists were killed and another three seriously wounded. He himself killed one terrorist.

In March 1952 he was in command of his platoon on patrol when he came upon an occupied bandit camp on the Waterfall Estate. Attacking instantly, his platoon killed one bandit and wounded two others.

In February 1953 he was in command of a small party from his platoon when it contacted and killed one terrorist.

Sergeant Healey has invariably displayed qualities of determination and resource of the highest order. His courage and leadership have been an inspiration to his platoon and company over a very long period.

Lance-Corporal J. C. Martin.—This young lance-corporal was the senior rank left alive or not seriously wounded in the leading un-armoured lorry of a convoy of three vehicles which was ambushed on the Ulu Caledonia Estate, North Selangor, on October 22, 1951, while conveying his platoon back to base on completion of a patrol. The senior officer and his platoon sergeant had been killed outright, his platoon commander had been severely wounded and, after a short time, only four other ranks, of whom one was already hit, remained alive or not badly wounded in the immediate area of his vehicle.

The enemy were a well-organised and well-led gang of bandits, at least 30 strong and armed with automatics, rifles and grenades. It was not long before the total strength of his platoon had been reduced by their fire to 16, mostly wounded, men.

In this desperate situation, Lance-Corporal Martin acted as a non-commissioned officer should. He did his best to take the responsibility of command over the four men remaining effective in his immediate area by word, action and example. He expended all his own ammunition and received some more from one of the wounded. He helped to drag wounded men to the safety of such cover as existed. When the enemy charged, Lance-Corporal Martin led the small arms fire which halted them.

Although he was himself badly hit and put out of action before the fight had gone on for long, Lance-Corporal Martin had helped to start a brave resistance which eventually forced the enemy to withdraw, leaving six dead and three of their weapons, and with the object of seizing the arms of his platoon completely frustrated.

Sergeant K. J. Wilde.—Sergeant Wilde has been an operational platoon sergeant since the arrival of the battalion in Malaya in April 1951, and for several periods, particularly within the last six months, has commanded a platoon without an officer. As such, he has shown himself to be a most able and efficient leader, fully capable of commanding a platoon on any operation.

He has taken part in many actions in Malaya. In one of these, on February 2, 1953, he was commanding No. 9 Platoon in a multi-ambush position. Two terrorists approached from the rear. The terrorists were engaged by one of the four groups and subsequently became involved with two further groups. The position of these groups made it possible for them to support each other mutually, and the initial success of the contact was largely due to the skill with which this N.C.O. had sited his ambush positions. Sergeant Wilde was not in the group which originally contacted the terrorists, but he became quickly engaged and it was almost entirely due to his aggressive handling of the contact and complete control of the situation that one terrorist was killed and the other captured. The captured terrorist was subsequently instrumental in obtaining for the unit seven kills in six contacts over a period of six days.

Sergeant Wilde has shown outstanding qualities of leadership, determination and keenness over a very long period. The morale of his platoon is particularly high, due to his forceful leadership.

APPENDIX C

Lists of officers on Active Service

With The 1st Battalion

MALAYA, 1951-1954

On First Deployment, April 1951

Commanding Officer	Lieut.-Colonel	A. Martyn
2nd-in-Command	Major	D. H. Andrews, M.C.
Adjutant	Captain	V. Dover, M.C.
Intelligence Officer	Lieutenant	J. R. Lygo
Quartermaster	Captain	A. E. Sivers, M.M.
R.S.M.	W.O.I	S. V. Stephens
Bandmaster	W.O.I	R. G. Watkins
R.Q.M.S.	W.O.II	J. E. Grubb

H.Q. Company

Coy. Com.	Major	G. P. Fawcett
Signals	Lieutenant	K. Dodson
Transport	Lieutenant	S. R. O'R. Shearburn
C.S.M.	W.O.II	T. Leigh

A Company

Coy. Com.	Major	A. J. M. Flint, M.B.E.
2nd-in-Command	Captain	J. B. Wilson
Pl. Com.	2nd Lieutenant	K. S. Beale
Pl. Com.	2nd Lieutenant	D. H. Woolstencroft
Pl. Com.	2nd Lieutenant	M. D. A. Gregson
C.S.M.	W.O.II	G. Tidey

B Company

Coy. Com.	Major	M. B. Rickcord
2nd-in-Command	Captain	K. M. Hunting
Pl. Com.	Lieutenant	B. C. H. Waters
Pl. Com.	2nd Lieutenant	P. R. Stock
Pl. Com.	2nd Lieutenant	P. S. Leigh
C.S.M.	W.O.II	C. Jackson

C Company

Coy. Com.	Major	P. E. Crook, O.B.E.
2nd-in-Command	Captain	E. A. Deed
Pl. Com.	Lieutenant	D. P. I. Campbell
Pl. Com.	2nd Lieutenant	H. A. L. Ferguson
Pl. Com.	2nd Lieutenant	G. W. H. Howlett
C.S.M.	W.O.II	A. Hills

D Company (Designate)

Coy. Com.	Major	E. C. Spurr
2nd-in-Command	Captain	T. V. Upton
Pl. Com.	2nd Lieutenant	R. D. Wilson
Pl. Com.	2nd Lieutenant	J. B. Bracewell-Milnes
Pl. Com.	2nd Lieutenant	M. D. C. Watkins
C.S.M.	W.O.II	A. Dallen

Support Company

Coy. Com.	Major	P. C. M. Buckle
Mortar Pl.	Lieutenant	J. D. Norton
M.M.G. Pl.	Lieutenant	J. S. Fletcher
Anti-Tank Pl.	Lieutenant	P. J. Goodwin
— :: —	2nd Lieutenant	T. A. Tilley
Pioneer Pl.	2nd Lieutenant	J. D. De Pury
C.S.M.	W.O.II	R. Nichols

Joined in Malaya

(Some names may have been omitted from this list)

2nd Lieutenant	J. P. Langhorne	May 1951
Captain	D. Ruffell	May 1951
Captain	M. F. Leonard (Middlesex)	Aug. 1951
Lieut.-Colonel	G. G. Elliott, D.S.O.	Jan. 1952
Captain	I. H. Roper, M.C.	Jan. 1952
2nd Lieutenant	C. E. Craven	Feb. 1952
2nd Lieutenant	H. C. Elwell	Feb. 1952
2nd Lieutenant	A. C. L. Halsall	Mar. 1952
Major	H. B. H. Waring	Apr. 1952
Major	A. L. A. Bishop (E. Surrey)	Apr. 1952
Captain	V. C. Abplanalp	Apr. 1952
Major	D. O. Faulkner	July 1952
Captain	D. S. Scull	July 1952
Captain	W. D. Allen	Aug. 1952
Captain	A. W. Franklin	Aug. 1952
Lieutenant	E. J. Marshall	Sep. 1952
Captain	H. A. Macmillan	Oct. 1952
2nd Lieutenant	R. W. Neve	Oct. 1952
Major	M. G. M. Archer, M.C.	Jan. 1953
Lieutenant	J. A. Scouller	Feb. 1953
Lieut.-Colonel	A. R. Fyler	Mar. 1953
Major	W. C. D. Crumplin	May 1953
Captain	P. Crook, M. C. (R. Fusiliers)	May 1953
Lieutenant	W. R. Wood	June 1953
2nd Lieutenant	C. L. Tarver	Aug. 1953
Major	R. K. Dowse	Aug. 1953
Major	J. H. Brock	Aug. 1953
2nd Lieutenant	M. R. M. Newall	Aug. 1953
Major	P. N. Elgood	Sep. 1953
Major	M. R. L. Grove, M.C.	Sep. 1953

National Service Officers Who Joined in Malaya

2nd Lieutenant	A. F. Trevett	May	1951
2nd Lieutenant	J. M. Taylor	July	1951
2nd Lieutenant	D. C. D. Reoch	July	1951
2nd Lieutenant	P. J. Kitteridge	Aug.	1951
2nd Lieutenant	G. T. Barnes	Dec.	1951
2nd Lieutenant	G. D. R. Smith	Feb.	1952
2nd Lieutenant	A. G. Jackson	July	1952
2nd Lieutenant	J. D. Lincoln	July	1952
2nd Lieutenant	D. W. Manning	July	1952
2nd Lieutenant	J. W. M. Blanch	Aug.	1952
2nd Lieutenant	C. D. T. Fitch	Nov.	1952
2nd Lieutenant	R. N. Young	Nov.	1952
2nd Lieutenant	A. B. Dunlop	Dec.	1952
2nd Lieutenant	R. K. Parker	May	1953
2nd Lieutenant	C. G. Fraser	Aug.	1953
2nd Lieutenant	E. Y. S. Bathurst	Sep.	1953
2nd Lieutenant	F. A. Follett-Smith	Sep.	1953
2nd Lieutenant	P. J. C. O'Donoghue	Sep.	1953
2nd Lieutenant	P. J. Morley-Jacob	Sep.	1953
2nd Lieutenant	M. V. Nyren	Sep.	1953
2nd Lieutenant	P. H. Sylvester	Oct.	1953

EGYPT AND CYPRUS, 1956-1959

Landed at Port Said and Went on to Cyprus

Commanding Officer	Lieut.-Colonel	P. C. M. Buckle
2nd-in-Command	Major	A. J. M. Flint, M.B.E.
Adjutant	Captain	K. Dodson
Asst. Adjutant	Captain	J. S. Fletcher
Intelligence Officer	Lieutenant	A. F. Heatly
Quartermaster	Major	A. G. Blake, M.B.E.
R.S.M.	W.O.I	J. E. Grubb, M.B.E.
R.Q.M.S.	W.O.II	G. V. I. Simpson

H.Q. Company

Coy. Com.	Major	T. V. Upton, M.B.E.
Adminstration	2nd Lieutenant	K. Cannell
Signals	Captain	R. W. Neve, M.C.
Transport	Captain	A. P. Mansfield
— :: —	2nd Lieutenant	J. Beeching
C.S.M.	W.O.II	A. G. Parker

A Company

Coy. Com.	Major	R. K. Dowse
2nd-in-Command	Captain	E. C. S. Osborne
Pl. Com.	2nd Lieutenant	A. G. Witheridge
Pl. Com.	2nd Lieutenant	W. J. Gibbs
Pl. Com.	2nd Lieutenant	J. Langhorne
C.S.M.	W.O.II	D. Baker

B Company

Coy. Com.	Major	C. F. Willis, M.B.E., T.D.
2nd-in-Command	Captain	D.P. I. Campbell
Pl. Com.	Lieutenant	E. A. Taylor
Pl. Com.	2nd Lieutenant	P. Hiscock
Pl. Com.	2nd Lieutenant	D. Parish
Supernumerary	2nd Lieutenant	P. S. Blunt
C.S.M.	W.O.II	J. H. Jones

C Company

Coy. Com.	Major	R. Butler, M.B.E., M.C.
2nd-in-Command	Captain	S. R. O'R. Shearburn
Pl. Com.	2nd Lieutenant	M. J. Smith
Pl. Com.	2nd Lieutenant	G. F. Warner
Pl. Com.	2nd Lieutenant	I. H. D. Tollemache
Supernumerary	2nd Lieutenant	S. M. Hoare
C.S.M.	W.O.II	K. Wilde, M.M.

D Company

Coy. Com.	Major	D. Monckton, M.C., T.D.
2nd-in-Command	Captain	D. Ruffell
Pl. Com.	2nd Lieutenant	C. D. B. Butler
Pl. Com.	2nd Lieutenant	M. A. Maberly
Pl. Com.	2nd Lieutenant	R. A. G. Hillier
C.S.M.	W.O.II	F. G. Bradshaw

Support Company

Coy. Com.	Major	M. R. Read, M.C.
Mortar Pl.	Captain	I. D. Pybus
—:—	2nd Lieutenant	N. A. Hallidie
M.M.G. Pl.	Captain	W. R. Wood
Anti-Tank Pl.	Lieutenant	R. J. Durtnell
Pioneer Pl.	Lieutenant	P. R. Butlin
C.S.M.	W.O.II	L. A. Warren

Attached

Paymaster	Major	A. K. Hind, T.D. (R.A.P.C.)
Medical Officer	Lieutenant	J. F. Walker (R.A.M.C.)

Joined in Cyprus

Captain	D. H. Woolstencroft	Dec. 1956
Major	M. G. M. Archer, M.C.	Mar. 1957
Captain	C. S. Clarke	Mar. 1957
Captain	J. A. Scouller	Mar. 1957
2nd Lieutenant	T. K. Colgate	Apr. 1957
2nd Lieutenant	C. G. Champion	June 1957
2nd Lieutenant	G. F. Cleaver	July 1957
2nd Lieutenant	N. C. Pearce	July 1957
Captain	H. A. Macmillan	Aug. 1957
Major	H. B. H. Waring	Aug. 1957
Captain	V. C. Abplanalp	Sep. 1957
Lieutenant	C. L. Tarver	Nov. 1957
Bt.-Lieut.-Col.	D. C. J. Manners	Feb. 1958
2nd Lieutenant	M. J. Clinch	Feb. 1958
Major	W. C. D. Crumplin	Mar. 1958
Major	I. A. Macmillan	Apr. 1958
Captain	J. D. Norton	June 1958
2nd Lieutenant	G. B. Bateman	Sep. 1958
Captain	P. J. Goodwin	Nov. 1958
Major	P. N. Elgood	Dec. 1958
2nd Lieutenant	J. C. Holman	Jan. 1959
2nd Lieutenant	R. H. Whitty	Jan. 1959

Captain	M. R. M. Newall	Feb. 1959
Captain	P. S. Leigh, M.C.	Feb. 1959
Captain	C. E. Craven	Mar. 1959
Bt.-Lieut.-Col.	D. H. Gwilliam, M.B.E.	Apr. 1959

National Service Officers Who Joined in Cyprus

2nd Lieutenant	W. G. Calcutt	Dec. 1956
2nd Lieutenant	S. E. Coningham	Feb. 1957
2nd Lieutenant	C. W. F. Meister	Mar. 1957
2nd Lieutenant	R. C. Robertson	June 1957
2nd Lieutenant	T. J. B. Locker	June 1957
2nd Lieutenant	W. G. Leckie	June 1957
2nd Lieutenant	J. D. Johnston	Aug. 1957
2nd Lieutenant	F. J. French	Mar. 1958
2nd Lieutenant	D. B. Evers	Apr. 1958
2nd Lieutenant	J. R. Govan	June 1958
2nd Lieutenant	A. J. Scouller	July 1958
2nd Lieutenant	J. B. Coles	Sep. 1958
2nd Lieutenant	P. F. Valpy	Dec. 1958
2nd Lieutenant	M. S. Barnes	June 1959

APPENDIX D

List of Home Guard Battalions

A LIST OF HOME GUARD BATTALIONS AFFILIATED TO THE QUEEN'S OWN, 1952-1956

11th Kent	Maidstone	Lieut.-Col. E. S. Kerr
12th/13th Kent	Gillingham	Lieut.-Col. H. Ewart-Biggs
14th Kent	Higham	Lieut.-Col. D. G. Cadic, M.B.E., T.D.
16th Kent	Gravesend	Lieut.-Col. E. A. Mole, J.P.
18th Kent	Greenhithe	Lieut.-Col. D. Seeley-Jones
20th Kent	Sevenoaks	Lieut.-Col. J. R. O. Warde, T.D., D.L.
21st/32nd Kent	Tonbridge	Lieut.-Col. R. V. Burke
22nd Kent	Tunbridge Wells	Lieut.-Col. S. T. Rew
24th Kent	West Malling	Lieut.-Col. W. O. H. Joynson
29th Kent	Headcorn	Lieut.-Col. H. G. Trouton
51st Kent	Bromley	Lieut.-Col. T. Kingsley Collett, C.B.E.
53rd Kent	Orpington	Lieut.-Col. D. Filshill
54th Kent	Chislehurst	Lieut.-Col. K. G. Livingstone
55th Kent	Penge	Lieut.-Col. W. E. Grey
56th Kent	Bexleyheath	Lieut.-Col. C. B. E. Grassley
57th Kent	Beckenham	Lieut.-Col. H. E. Tunnicliffe, M.C.

APPENDIX E

The Last Order of Battle

1st Battalion

Commanding Officer	Lieut.-Colonel	D. H. Gwilliam, M.B.E.
2nd-in-Command	Major	E. G. Woodman, M.C.
Adjutant	Captain	I. D. Pybus
Intelligence Off.	Lieutenant	P. Hiscock
Quartermaster	Lieutenant	E. J. W. Hoggart
R.S.M.	W.O.1	A. G. Parker, M.B.E.
Bandmaster	W.O.1	R. G. Watkins, M.B.E.
R.Q.M.S.	W.O.11	R. J. Palmer

H.Q. Company

Company Com.	Major	D. E. Blum
2nd-in-Command	Captain	P. J. Goodwin
Administration	2nd Lieutenant	G. A. Dawkins
Signals	Captain	G. F. Cleaver
Transport	Captain	L. A. Mannering
C.S.M.	W.O.11	B. Simmonite

A Company

Company Com.	Major	R. G. Winstanley
2nd-in-Command	Captain	P. S. Leigh, M.C.
Pl. Com.	Lieutenant	J. C. Holman
Pl. Com.	Lieutenant	J. E. Gerelli
Pl. Com.	2nd Lieutenant	C. W. G. Thompson
C.S.M.	Colour-Sergeant	G. E Levett

B Company

Company Com.	Major	D. S. Scull
2nd-in-Command	Captain	M. R. M. Newall
Pl. Com.	2nd Lieutenant	R. J. Pickering
Pl. Com.	2nd Lieutenant	B. K. Donovan
C.S.M.	W.O.11	T. N. Ross Gower

C Company

Company Com.	Major	A. W. Franklin
2nd-in-Command	Major	E. C. S. Osborne
Pl. Com.	Lieutenant	J. B. Coles
Pl. Com.	2nd Lieutenant	R. F. Schooling
Pl. Com.	2nd Lieutenant	C. J. Pearson
C.S.M.	W.O.11	J. Heyfron

D Company

Disbanded owing to the run-down in personnel.

Support Company

Company Com.	Captain	C. T. F. West (The Buffs)
Mortar Pl.	Lieutenant	M. J. Smith
M.M.G. Pl.	Lieutenant	C. G. Champion
Anti-Tank Pl.	Lieutenant	N. C. Pearce
Pioneer Pl.	Sergeant	H. Coleman
C.S.M.	W.O.11	L. W. Spalding

Attached

Paymaster	Major	A. K. Hind, T.D. (R.A.P.C.)
Medical Officer	Captain	P. E. Moffit (R.A.M.C.)
Education Officer	Lieutenant	H. H. G. Nisbet (R.A.E.C.)

APPENDIX F

Memorials to The Queen's Own

MEMORIALS to officers and other ranks of The Queen's Own, who died on active service and in peacetime, are scattered over the world. Some of them were set up by their comrades, others by a grateful community or by a military formation.

The oldest of these memorials on record is in the porch of the English Church at Biarritz. It is a tablet to the memory of the 34 members of The 50th Regiment who lost their lives in South-West France during the last seven months of the Peninsular War (October 1813 to April 1814).

The next oldest is a stone and brass tomb outside Fort William in Strand Road, Calcutta. The inscription on it is: "To the officers and men of His Majesty's and the Honourable East India Company's Troops who fell in the victorious actions at Maharajpur and Punniar, 1843." The list of names includes 10 of The 50th who were killed at Punniar.

A figure of Britannia and a plaque were placed by their comrades on the north wall of the nave in Canterbury Cathedral in memory of the 199 officers and men of The 50th who fell in the Sutlej Campaign in 1845-1846. The Crimea Memorial of The 50th is also in Canterbury Cathedral.

A stained-glass window was erected in the church at Loodiana, India, to commemorate the 82 men, women and children of The 50th who lost their lives when the European barracks in Loodiana cantonment were blown down by a great storm on May 20th, 1846. (See *The Queen's Own Gazette* for August 1937.)

The Crimea Memorial of The 97th (Earl of Ulster's) Regiment is in Winchester Cathedral. It is a stained-glass window, above which hang the Colours carried by The 97th at Sevastopol. Beneath the window are four tablets. On one is the inscription: "The above window is dedicated by the officers now serving and those who have lately served in The 97th or Earl of Ulster's Regiment to the memory of the officers, non-commissioned officers, drummers and privates of the corps who lost their lives when the regiment occupied the Piraeus, Greece, in conjunction with the French in 1854 and did duty in the trenches at the siege and fall of Sevastopol, 1855." Under this tablet is another of similar size giving the names of the 10 officers who died. The third tablet has on it some texts from the Bible. The fourth shows that the number of soldiers who died was 527, and gives the cause of death.

One of the officers of The 97th who was killed at Sevastopol was Major A. F. Welsford. An archway erected to his memory stands in St. Paul's Cemetery in Halifax, Nova Scotia, where he was born. This memorial was set up by the local community.

The most remote memorials connected with the regiment are the two in North Island, New Zealand. One is a hatchment in St. Mary's Church, New Plymouth, which commemorates the members of The 50th Regiment who fell while fighting the Maoris in the province of Taranaki in 1865-1866. The other is a stone cross alongside the "Veterans' Steps" at Wanganui to the memory of the 11 soldiers of The 50th who were killed in the action at Nukumaru in January 1865. (See *The Queen's Own Gazette* for March and April 1952.)

After 1881, when The 50th and 97th Regiments became the 1st and 2nd Battalions The Queen's Own Royal West Kent Regiment, the name of every member of the regiment who lost his life on active service was recorded in All Saints' Church, Maidstone, on a memorial, on a plaque or in a Book of Remembrance.

The first regimental memorial to be placed in All Saints' Church was a window to the 79 all ranks who lost their lives in Egypt and the Sudan, 1882-1886. This was followed by a memorial screen to the 17 members of the 1st Battalion who died during the Punjab Frontier Campaign, 1897-1898. Next was a plaque to the three other ranks of the 1st Battalion who died during the Aden Expedition of 1901. Then came a memorial window and plaque to the 116 all ranks who fell in the War in South Africa, 1900-1902. There are also tablets in the church in memory of the three officers and one sergeant who died on active service in East and West Africa between 1900 and 1904.

Three other South African War Memorials concerning the regiment were set up besides that in All Saints' Church: a monument at Harrismith in the Orange Free State to the 8th Division (Rundle's Greyhounds), in which the 2nd Battalion served; a marble tablet in the Lady Chapel of Rochester Cathedral to "the soldiers of the County of Kent;" and a plaque in St. Alfege's Church at Greenwich to the nine other ranks of the 2nd Volunteer Battalion who died.

The Roll of Honour of The Queen's Own for the Great War, 1914-1918, and Afghanistan 1919 contained 6,851 names. It was decided to record them in a Book of Remembrance, which was placed in All Saints' Church in July 1938. In addition, a Regimental Cenotaph was erected in Brenchley Gardens, Maidstone. It is a replica, rather smaller in size, of the Cenotaph in Whitehall and was designed by the same architect, Sir Edwin Lutyens.

Other memorials to the regiment for the Great War are a Regimental Banner in St. George's Memorial Church, Ypres, to those of The Queen's Own who fell in the Ypres Salient; and a panel in the chapel of the Royal Military Academy, Sandhurst. There are a cenotaph in Lewisham High Street and a Memorial Window in St. Laurence's Church, Catford, to those of the 11th Battalion who lost their lives. A stone memorial was erected in the grounds of Holly Hedge House, Blackheath, to those of the 20th Battalion The London Regiment who fell. There is a tablet in the Parish Church at Shoreham-by-Sea, Sussex, to the Service Battalions who trained in the area. A memorial in the church at Mons commemorates the British regiments which fought there in the early days of the war; the 1st Battalion was there. A window was placed in the Mesopotamian Memorial Church at Baghdad in memory of the members of the 2nd Battalion who fell during the Mesopotamian Campaign.

Two of the many divisional memorials which were erected for the 1914-1918 War had a special significance for the regiment. These are the memorial in Trones Wood to the 18th Division, in which the 7th Battalion served; and the one at Flers to the 41st Division (10th and 11th Battalions).

After the 2nd Battalion left Palestine in 1939, an oak lectern was unveiled in the chapel at Peninsula Barracks, Haifa, in memory of the 11 other ranks of the unit who had been killed in action or had died of disease in Palestine. This lectern was brought to England in 1948 and, at the time of writing, is at the Regimental Headquarters (Increment) of The Queen's Own Buffs at Maidstone.

There are seven known memorials to members of the regiment who died at overseas stations in peacetime. The earliest is in the Military Cemetery at Newcastle, Jamaica, to the two officers and 14 other ranks of The 97th Regiment who died in Jamaica in 1848-1851 and 1874-1875. The next is a painting of St. Luke and a plaque in the Garrison Church in Tigne Barracks, Malta, to the 12 other ranks of the 1st Battalion who died on the island in 1902 and 1904-1906. The third is a brass plaque in the Garrison Church in Tanglin Barracks at Singapore to the officer and six other ranks of the 2nd Battalion who died there in 1906-1908. There is a stone cross in St. Sepulchre's Cemetery at Poona to the 11 other ranks of the 1st Battalion who died while serving in that station in 1922-1927. A cross of gold was placed on Holy Trinity Church at Bangalore and a brass tablet inside the church to eight men of the 1st Battalion, 1928-1932. Plaques were placed in the Garrison Churches at Trimulgherry and Karachi to six of the 1st Battalion, 1932-1936, and to two of the 1st Battalion, 1936-1937, respectively.

Some memorials to members of the regiment who died in peacetime are in All Saints' Church, Maidstone. These are tablets to Colonel C. H. Browne, the first C.O. of the 2nd Battalion; to Major N. H. Leckie, who was commissioned into The 97th in 1872, retired from the regiment in 1889 and left a bequest to The Queen's Own; to Lieutenant S. J. Barton, who was R.S.M. of the 1st Battalion during the Punjab Frontier Campaign and later Quartermaster of the 1st Volunteer Battalion; to Brigadier-General A. Martyn, who commanded the 1st Battalion from March 1912 to October 1914; and to Colonels H. D. Buchanan-Dunlop and W. V. Palmer, both of whom were Chairmen of The Queen's Own Past and Present Association.

There is a memorial tablet in Lichfield Cathedral to Lieutenant-Colonel P. J. Petit, of The 50th Regiment, who died at Lichfield in 1852. It was erected by the officers of The 50th in remembrance of his gallant services at the Battle of Punniar and during the Sutlej Campaign.

In Winchester Cathedral there is a memorial tablet to Colonel

William West Turner, of The 97th Regiment, who died at Naples in 1871. It was erected by his brother officers.

A memorial plaque in St. Laurence's Church, Catford, commemorates Lieutenant-Colonel A. C. Corfe, who commanded the 11th Battalion from September 1916 till September 1917 and in February and March 1918. The plaque was set up by his comrades.

In July 1951 a Book of Remembrance was placed in All Saints' Church, Maidstone, in memory of the 1,678 members of The Queen's Own who gave their lives in the Second World War, 1939-1945.

Five memorials commemorate members of the regiment who died during that war. Two of them are at Kohima—a wooden cross erected by their comrades to the 61 of the 4th Battalion who were killed in the Defence of Kohima in April 1944, and a monolith to those of the 5th Indian Division who fell in the Defence and Relief of Kohima from March to June 1944. Another, at Griefenburg in Austria, is a cross of pinewood dedicated to those of the 6th Battalion who lost their lives in North Africa, Sicily and Italy; their names were painted on it, but have become illegible. In St. Paul's Anglican Cathedral in Valletta, Malta, inscribed wooden panelling commemorates the units who served in the Defence of Malta from June 1940 to May 1943; the 2nd Battalion was there. And a pew of English oak in the nave of the Royal Military Academy Chapel, Sandhurst, commemorates the officers of the regiment who died, 1939-1945.

In a quarry on Lundy Island is a memorial stone to Lance-Corporal J. P. Harman, who won a posthumous Victoria Cross with the 4th Battalion at Kohima. Harman's father owned the island for some time.

The name of 6387016 Lance-Corporal E. R. Lawrence (attached 10 Commando) is on the Commonwealth Memorial at Bayeaux. That memorial commemorates those of the Commonwealth Land Forces who fell in the assault on the Normandy Beaches or in the advance to the Seine in 1944 and have no known graves.

Other Commonwealth Memorials with Queen's Own names on them are at Athens, Brookwood, Cassino, Dunkirk, El Alamein, Groesbeek, Medjez-el-Bab, Reichswald and Rangoon. (See section 1 of chapter 1 and section 1 of chapter 3 above.)

The last Queen's Own Memorial was a Book of Remembrance in All Saints' Church, Maidstone, for the officer who was killed in an ambush in Malaya in 1949; the private who died of wounds in Korea in 1950; the colour-sergeant who died in Kenya in 1953; the two officers and eight other ranks who lost their lives on active service with the 1st Battalion in Malaya in 1951-1954; and the private who died while serving with that battalion in Cyprus during the emergency, 1956-1959. The names of the 11 other ranks of the 2nd Battallion who died in Palestine in 1938 are also inscribed in that Book.

APPENDIX G

A brief history of "The Queens's Own Gazette"

THE *Queen's Own Gazette* was first published on January 1, 1875 as the monthly journal of The 50th (The Queen's Own) Regiment. It was printed at Regimental Headquarters at Ship Street Barracks, Dublin, by Corporal Hunt on a printing press which had, it seems, been bought for the purpose. Lieutenant Brock was the editor. Lieutenant-Colonel Lock was the commanding officer.

Five months before, on August 1, 1874, the two Depot companies of The 50th, together with those of The 97th Regiment, had been sent to Maidstone to establish a permanent Depot. This gave The 50th a fixed home, which till then it had lacked. Even so, the printing press was not sent to the Depot when the regiment changed stations, but was taken with it when it moved from Dublin to Kinsale (on the south coast of Ireland), from Kinsale to Edinburgh Castle, and thence to Colchester. The printer of the Q.O.G. was changed twice; Hunt handed over to Sergeant Richardson at Kinsale in February 1877, and Private Taylor took over the press at Edinburgh in May 1878.

The early numbers of the Q.O.G. contained an editorial column; a personal column, usually known as " Births, Marriages and Deaths "; and an article on general military matters, such as Regimental Facings or Regimental Marches. For several months the Historical Records of The 50th were published as a serial. Mention was occasionally made of The 97th Regiment, with which The 50th had been linked for the purposes of enlistment and service since April 1, 1873.

L

On the formation of County Regiments on July 1, 1881, The 50th and The 97th became the 1st and 2nd Battalions, and the West Kent Light Infantry Militia the 3rd and 4th Battalions of The Queen's Own (Royal West Kent Regiment). There were also three Volunteer battalions in the regiment. Yet the Q.O.G. was the journal of the 1st Battalion only, and the printing press was taken from Colchester to Aldershot when that battalion moved there in November 1881.

But when, in August 1882, the 1st Battalion was mobilized and sailed to Egypt as part of the Expeditionary Force which quelled Arabi's rebellion, Private Taylor took the printing press to the Depot. The adjutant of the Depot (then Captain J. G. Smith) became the editor of the Q.O.G., and the paper became the journal of The Queen's Own (Royal West Kent Regiment).

When Taylor was discharged from the Army in August 1884, a successor could not be found to operate the printing press. The task of producing the Q.O.G. was given to *The Maidstone and Kent County Standard* as a temporary measure.

There were other setbacks. In April 1887 some of the Depot staff were unexpectedly ordered to join the 2nd Battalion at Chatham, and two civilians helped to produce the Q.O.G., which that month consisted of only a single sheet. For five months, from November 1887 to March 1888 inclusive, the journal was not published at all owing to lack of support.

The Q.O.G. re-appeared in its usual form in April 1888, when it was set up by Corporal Weeks on the regimental printing press at the Depot. Weeks handed over to Sergeant Hickey in June 1889. The next printer was Lance-Corporal Gibbs. While he was in charge of the press, the type was found to be worn out. New type was bought from Messrs. Harrild and Sons of London in July 1890. Gibbs was relieved by Corporal Hibbert in December, 1893.

Then a calamity occurred. At 4 a.m. on February 21 1896, the wooden building, in which were the Printing Office, the Quartermaster's Stores and the Tailor's Shop, was seen by a sentry to be on fire. It was two hours before the flames were quenched. Some of the property of the 3rd Battalion officers' mess and some of the Militia officers' kit were destroyed. Back numbers of the Q.O.G. were damaged by water. Although much of the type was said to have been saved, the journal was not printed in barracks again. A contract for the printing of the Q.O.G. was made with Messrs. Dickinson of Maidstone. The contract was transferred in 1897 to the *Kent Messenger,* with which firm it remained until the journal ceased to be produced.

Each monthly edition of the journal now consisted of 10 or 12 pages. Besides Promotions, Appointments, Births, Marriages and Deaths, it contained correspondence from the 1st and 2nd Battalions, news of the Volunteer battalions and, in the summer, accounts of the annual training of the Militia. After the War in South Africa (1899-1902), company correspondence began to appear.

During the Great War of 1914-18, the Q.O.G. was one of the few regimental magazines to be produced without interruption. This was mainly due to Colonel Brock, who had been the first editor. He returned to the editor's chair early in 1915 and kept the journal going until the end of the conflict. Free copies were sent to many of the hospitals in which personnel of The Queen's Own lay wounded.

After the 1914-18 War the editorial pen was once more taken up by the adjutant of the Depot. In 1920 this appointment was held by Captain Palmer, under whose editorship the Q.O.G. expanded to 20 pages. In addition, by registering the journal with The Association of Regimental Magazines in October 1921, he obtained for the Q.O.G. Fund a regular income from advertisements.

During the Second World War there were many difficulties to contend with. Not the least was the blue pencil of the Censor. During the latter part of the war the paper shortage was so acute that the Q.O.G. was published only once a quarter. The monthly issue was resumed in January 1946. Thereafter the editor was Lieutenant-Colonel Eason who, as a retired officer, was the Administrative Officer at Regimental Headquarters.

Owing to the amalgamation of The Queen's Own Royal West Kent Regiment and The Buffs (Royal East Kent Regiment) on March 1 1961, *The Queen's Own Gazette,* as such, appeared for the last time in February 1961. Its successor, *Invicta, The Journal of The Queen's Own Buffs, The Royal Kent Regiment,* was first published in the following month. It was similar to the Q.O.G. in size and lay-out, contained all its regular features, and was printed by the *Kent Messenger.*

The Queen's Own Gazette was not the first regimental journal to be published. That distinction probably belongs to *The Dragon,* the magazine of The Buffs, which first appeared in 1874. But the Q.O.G. seems to have had the longest continuous existence. For *The Dragon* was not published for seven years between 1879 and 1886, nor from 1914 to 1919.

APPENDIX H

Nelson and The Queen's Own

EACH year on Trafalgar Day, October 21, a wreath is laid at the foot of Nelson's Column in London on behalf of the 1st Battalion of the regiment. This is done because The 50th (West Kent) Regiment once served under Nelson. The custom began in 1922, at the suggestion of the Navy League. Normally the wreath is laid by members of the London Branch of the Regimental Association.

The story of The 50th's connection with Nelson began at the end of 1793, when Admiral Lord Hood, the Commander-in-Chief of the British Mediterranean Fleet, decided to assist the Corsicans to throw off the yoke of the French.

There were French garrisons in three towns in Corsica—San Fiorenzo on the north coast, Bastia on the north-east, and Calvi on the north-west coast. Hood's ships were anchored in Hyeres Bay; aboard them were some British troops, who had just been evacuated from Toulon. The 50th Regiment arrived in the bay on December 31 from Gibraltar, where it had been stationed for over nine years.

Hood weighed anchor on January 24, 1794, for the Gulf of Fiorenzo, where he intended to set up the base for his expedition. On February 7, Major-General D. Dundas disembarked about 1,400 men and two light guns on the western shore of the gulf, and occupied a hill overlooking Martello Tower. On the 8th two ships bombarded the tower from the gulf, while the light guns battered it from the hill. After a red-hot shot had set fire to some rubbish on the ramparts, the garrison surrendered.

Two miles farther up the bay was Convention Redoubt. Against it six heavy guns, which had been dragged by sailors to the heights commanding it, opened fire on February 16. Next evening the troops delivered an assault in two columns, which advanced in perfect silence. The column led by Lieutenant-Colonel (later Sir John) Moore was the first to reach the work. The French stood firm. When the other column arrived, The 50th dashed in with the bayonet and the redoubt was captured with the loss of barely 50 casualties.

Two days later the British occupied the town of San Fiorenzo. the French garrison having withdrawn to Bastia.

While the base was being established, General Dundas sent a detachment to a pass in the ridge which barred the way to Bastia. On February 23 he himself ascended the ridge to reconnoitre the defences of that town. He saw four masonry forts on the land side; several batteries faced the sea. He decided that an attack on Bastia would be too hazardous without reinforcements, and that the town should be blockaded by land and sea until starvation compelled its garrison to surrender.

Captain Horatio Nelson was already blockading the north-east coast with a small naval squadron. Landing 60 sailors from his line-of-battle ship Agamemnon, he had captured Miomo, a village three miles north of Bastia, thereby inducing the Corsicans in the area to declare openly for the British. At the end of February the Agamemnon and two frigates bombarded the shore batteries for two hours, causing considerable damage. Emboldened by these successes, Nelson urged Lord Hood to attack Bastia.

Against the advice of Dundas, Hood sailed round to the north-east coast and landed a force of seamen and marines, 1,200 strong, at Miomo. Nelson was in command of the sailors. On April 11 this naval force opened fire on Bastia with 13 guns from a hill 2,500 yards north of the citadel. The bombardment had little effect because the range was too great. A month passed, while the army lay idle at San Fiorenzo. At length, reinforcements having reached the base, the troops marched for Bastia on May 19. Before they arrived. the garrison surrendered through lack of provisions. The soldiers occupied the town.

After Nelson had supervised their embarkation at Bastia, the troops sailed round Cape Corse in the Agamemnon, the Dolphin and the Gordon. The convoy was under Nelson's command. The troops landed on June 19 at Port Agro, an inlet three miles south-west of Calvi.

Calvi stands on a peninsula formed by a ridge of rocky hills. It was strongly fortified. The most formidable outworks were Fort Monteciesco and Fort Mozzello. Lieutenant-General Charles Stuart, who was now in command of the troops, decided to set up one battery to silence Monteciesco, and another to cover the construction of a gun-position 750 yards from Mozzello. With immense labour, 130 sailors under Nelson dragged 25 heavy guns up rugged cliffs to the batteries, where they manned all but three of the guns.

The bombardment of Monteciesco began on July 4. It inflicted much damage. On the 6th, under cover of a feint attack, the gun-position opposite Mozzello was established. For 10 days a destructive cannonade was exchanged. The French fire was remarkably accurate. On the 12th a round-shot struck the parapet of a battery which Nelson was directing, so that his face was badly bruised by gravel. Although he was off duty for only one day, this "little hurt", as he described it, caused the loss of sight of his right eye.

By July 18 a breach in the wall of Fort Mozzello was practicable. The assault was fixed for an hour before daylight on the following day. During the night, The 50th constructed a new battery 300 yards from the fort, and, with The 51st Regiment, took post there in reserve. At a signal The 1st (Royal Scots) and The 30th (East Lancashire) Regiments, under Colonel Moore, stormed the fort, while The 18th (Royal Irish) made for Fountain Battery on the left. Both works were carried with slight loss.

General Stuart then offered terms of surrender to Calvi, but the town refused to capitulate. So some heavy guns were dragged to a position nearer the walls, whence they opened fire on July 31. Stuart again offered terms, and the garrison agreed to surrender on August 10.

In the operations against Calvi the British losses were about 100. In addition for the last three weeks of the siege they had much sickness, with two-thirds of the soldiers in hospital. Those who continued at duty were exhausted by the labour and the heat. In his diary Moore wrote: "Perhaps there was never so much work done by so few men in the same space of time."

So the French were driven from Corsica, and the British gained a valuable naval base in the Mediterranean—for a time.

In the autumn of 1796 France formed an alliance with Spain. Threatened by such a formidable alliance, the British resolved that they could not maintain a garrison in Corsica. The evacuation of the island was supervised by Nelson. The 50th embarked on October 19 at Ajaccio, of which it had been the garrison, and sailed to Elba. Thence, a few months later, the regiment returned to Gibraltar.

APPENDIX J

The Queen's Own Past and Present Association

THE Queen's Own Past and Present Association was founded with the title The Queen's Own Old Comrades' Association in July 1911.

Seven years before that, another association had been formed in the regiment, namely The Association of Sergeants. Its membership included all warrant officers and sergeants, past and present, of the Line, Militia and Volunteer battalions.

At the annual dinner of The Association of Sergeants in July 1911, a proposal was made by ex-R.S.M. W. R. Brown that an Old Comrades' Association to include all ranks should be formed in the regiment. The idea was warmly welcomed, and a committee of past and present senior officers and other ranks met at the Golden Cross Hotel in London on July 22, 1911, to draw up rules.

The committee decided that membership should be open to all past members of the Line battalions, to all serving Regulars with seven or more years' service, and to all ranks of the auxiliary battalions who had been on active service with the regiment; that the annual subscription should be one shilling (five shillings for officers); that a dinner should be held each year in London on Cup Final Night; that the committee should be empowered to make grants to The Regimental Compassionate Fund, which till then had been supported solely by the officers; that the Colonel of the Regiment should be invited to be president; that Colonel C. E. C. B. Harrison should be chairman; and that the adjutant of the Depot should be secretary and treasurer.

By the end of 1911, some 250 members had been enrolled for The Queen's Own Old Comrades' Association, and a badge and a membership card had been designed. In January 1913, membership was extended to include all serving Regulars.

The first annual dinner was at Victoria Mansions Restaurant in Victoria Street on April 20, 1912, when about 120 were there. The second dinner, on April 19, 1913, was at Cannon Street Hotel; 160 members attended out of the 517 who had then joined. In April 1914 the dinner was at the Horseshoe Hotel in Tottenham Court Road.

The dinners were suspended during the Great War, 1914-1919.

The annual dinners were resumed on April 3, 1920, when 116 members assembled at Anderton's Hotel in Fleet Street. Colonel Harrison said that at the end of 1919 there had been more than 900 members, but because many of them had been demobilised and had not renewed their subscriptions, the effective strength was then less than 250. He considered that, as much work was required to get the association flourishing, a new committee should be formed, particularly because the adjutant of the Depot was unable to devote enough time to the secretarial duties.

A new committee was elected as follows: chairman, Brigadier-General E. A. W. S. Grove; secretary, Captain J. Douglas Burrows; treasurer, Mr. (ex-sergeant) E. G. Free; representatives from each of the Regular and Territorial battalions and also from each Service battalion raised during the Great War.

That committee met at Anderton's Hotel two weeks later and decided that the officer commanding the Depot and the R.S.M.s of the Regular and Territorial battalions should be co-opted to the committee; that all ranks of the Territorial and Service battalions should be eligible for membership; and that life membership should be introduced at 50/- for officers and 10/- for other ranks.

For the Burial of the Unknown Warrior on November 11, 1920, one ticket was allotted to the association for the service in Westminster Abbey, two tickets for the procession from Victoria Station to the Cenotaph in Whitehall, and three tickets for the ex-servicemen's procession from the Embankment to the Cenotaph. A wreath was laid at the Cenotaph in memory of all ranks of the regiment who had laid down their lives, 1914-1918.

The first branch of the association was at Penge and Beckenham. At a meeting of the past and present members of the local company of the 5th Battalion (T.A.) at the drill hall in Parish Lane, Penge, on December 4, 1920, the following resolution was passed: "That this meeting is in favour of the formation of a branch of The Old Comrades' Association for all those in the district who have served or are serving in the regiment." Captain Burrows attended the meeting and spoke of the advantages of membership.

Similar meetings at the drill halls at Dartford in January 1921 and at Bromley in March 1921 resolved to form branches at Dartford and Bromley respectively.

The Penge and Beckenham branch did not remain in existence for long.

The Bromley branch, as first constituted, also had a short life. But it was revived on November 4, 1931, with close links with the serving members of the 5th Battalion. Meetings were resumed at the drill hall in East Street.

Meanwhile the officers of the 8th (Service) Battalion had been holding annual dinners since December 1919. The first reunion for all ranks of that battalion was at Anderton's Hotel on April 30, 1921. The officers' dinners and all ranks' reunions of the 8th Battalion continued each year until 1939 inclusive. In April 1938 their wartime flag was taken into use as their Standard. The officers' dinners were resumed after the 1939-45 War.

The Chatham branch was formed in February 1922, but it soon lapsed. It was re-constituted in November 1935. Meetings were at the drill hall in Boundary Road. A branch Standard was presented on July 26, 1936.

The annual dinners of The Old Comrades' Association in April 1921 and April 1922 were at Anderton's Hotel. At the latter, it was decided that the next dinner should be at Maidstone during the Kent Cricket Week. It was also agreed that the association should be affiliated to the British Legion.

Captain Burrows resigned in January 1923. Captain A. Howe took over as secretary.

The 7th annual dinner of the association was at the Corn Exchange, Maidstone, on Saturday July 14, 1923, when 130 members attended. Some of them slept at the Depot that night, and on the Sunday morning the members mustered on the square and marched to Brenchley Gardens, where the Colonel of the Regiment placed a wreath at the Regimental Cenotaph. Wreaths were also laid on behalf of the 1st and 2nd Battalions and the Depot.

After the parade had returned to barracks, a general meeting of The Association of Sergeants took place. The meeting resolved that the funds of that association should be handed over to The Old Comrades' Association and that The Association of Sergeants should cease to exist.

The 8th annual dinner of the O.C.A. was at Anderton's Hotel on Cup Final Night in April 1924. The attendance was 86.

There is no record of the first reunion dinner of the 7th (Service) Battalion. Its second dinner was at the Chanticleer Hotel, London, on March 14, 1925. Thereafter the dinner took place annually until 1935 inclusive.

The 9th annual dinner of the association was in the gymnasium at the Depot on Saturday July 11, 1925. Next day the members marched with the troops of the Depot to All Saints' Church for Divine Service. The Mayor and Corporation of Maidstone were present. From the church, the parade marched to Brenchley Gardens for a memorial service at the Regimental Cenotaph. Among the wreaths laid was one by His Worship the Mayor. After lunch in barracks, there was a general meeting of the association.

Brigadier-General Grove resigned as chairman at that meeting. Colonel G. W. Maunsell took over.

For the next seven years the annual dinners of the association were alternately on Cup Final Night in London and on the Saturday of the Kent Cricket Week at Maidstone. When they were at Maidstone, a Sunday programme as outlined above was carried out.

The Maidstone branch was formed on February 3, 1928. Meetings were at the "Castle", of which ex-R.S.M. J. H. Outten was the proprietor, until December 1933. They were then transferred to the sergeants' mess at the Depot. A Standard was presented to the branch by the Colonel of the Regiment on July 14, 1935. Maidstone was the first branch to have a Standard.

The 11th (Service) Battalion Association was formed on January 27. 1932. It became affiliated to The Old Comrades' Association in July 1933. It held both a reunion dinner and a general meeting in London annually, and also a memorial service in St. Laurence's Church, Catford, on Remembrance Sunday each year till 1939. These were resumed after the 1939-1945 War.

Major W. V. Palmer, then commanding the Depot, became secretary of The Old Comrades' Association in January 1932. For the next 17 years the officer commanding the Depot acted as secretary.

Mr. Free, who had been treasurer of the association for 12 years, died in September 1932. He was succeeded by Warrant Officer M. Stroud, then R.S.M. of the Depot. Stroud was followed by Captain A. Howe (October 1934) and Captain (Q.M.) S. E. Brooks (July 1938).

The committee of the association resolved in November 1932 that, instead of an annual dinner, a reunion should be held at Maidstone each year during the Kent Cricket Week.

The title of the association was changed to The Queen's Own Past and Present Association at a committee meeting at Anderton's Hotel in April 1933. Another decision was that members who had paid ten annual subscriptions should be life members. The subscription for other ranks was raised to 2/-. Except in special cases, only members of the association would in future receive assistance from the Regimental Compassionate Fund.

The 1st Reunion of The Past and Present Association took place in July 1933. After assembling by battalions on the Depot square the parade, 600 strong, marched to Brenchley Gardens, where a memorial service was held and wreaths were laid at the Regimental Cenotaph. The Mayor and Corporation of Maidstone were there. The parade then returned to the Depot, where some 450 had lunch in the drill shed. In the afternoon, various entertainments were organised.

A short service in All Saints' Church was included in the morning programme for the Reunion from 1934 onwards.

The 6th (Service) Battalion Association was inaugurated at a dinner at the White Hart Hotel, Bromley, on November 18, 1933. The dinner was subsequently held each year until 1939 inclusive.

When His Royal Highness The Duke of Kent became Colonel-in-

Chief of the regiment in March 1935, he graciously consented to be Patron of The Past and Present Association.

The Tonbridge and Tunbridge Wells branch was formed on July 24, 1935. Meetings were in the drill hall in Bank Street, Tonbridge. A Standard was presented to the branch during the 4th Reunion on July 26, 1936.

The 20th London O.C.A. became affiliated to The Past and Present Association in July 1935. It had been formed after the Service battalions were demobilised in 1919. Meetings were in the sergeants' mess at Holly Hedge House, Blackheath. An annual dinner was held in London on the Saturday nearest to Armistice Day (November 11), and a memorial service at Holly Hedge House on Remembrance Sunday.

Two branches were formed in 1936. The first was at Shorncliffe on January 22. Meetings were usually in the Reading Room in Napier Barracks, where the 2nd Battalion was then quartered. The branch Standard was dedicated at the 5th Reunion in July 1937.

The other branch formed in 1936 was in London. It was inaugurated at a meeting at the Central London Recruiting Depot in Whitehall on March 25. Colonel Maunsell (chairman of the P. and P.) presided. The first committee meeting was on April 8, when rules were drawn up. The first meeting of the branch took place on April 27 at the Chevrons Club in St. George's Square, Victoria, where subsequently meetings were held monthly. A Standard was presented to the branch on July 26, 1936, during the 4th Reunion.

A room in the "Brown Bear" at Deptford was placed at the disposal of the London members living in that area, and the Deptford Social Club was formed in October 1937.

At the Coronation of King George VI in May 1937, all branches of the association were represented. At the Coronation Ex-Servicemen's Review in Hyde Park, 203 members and six Standards were on parade.

Colonel Maunsell handed over the duties of chairman to Colonel H. D. Buchanan-Dunlop on November 10, 1937.

The Gravesend branch started in September 1938. It met at the Terminus Hotel. The branch Standard was dedicated at a drumhead service in Milton Barracks in April 1939.

Soon after war was declared in September 1939, most of the branches suspended their meetings because it was too difficult to get home at night during the "blackout". The Gravesend branch continued its meetings, with a small attendance, till the end of 1940. The London branch and its Social Club at Deptford held some meetings on Sunday mornings during the winter of 1939-1940. The London branch reverted to evening meetings in the spring of 1940 until the Chevrons Club was damaged by bombs in the autumn. It then met once or twice at the "Green Man" at Putney Heath. But war work and Home Guard duties cut down the attendance so much that it, too, suspended its meetings until the end of the war.

★ ★ ★

The first post-war general meeting of The Past and Present Association took place at the Depot on August 25 1945. Colonel Buchanan-Dunlop said that the chairmanship should be assumed by a younger man. Colonel W. V. Palmer took over.

One by one the branches resumed their meetings. The first was the London branch at the renovated Chevrons Club in April 1945. The next was the Gravesend branch in August 1945. The Chatham and Shorncliffe branches held their first post-war meetings in November 1945. The rest followed suit in due course.

The Deptford Social Club became the Deptford and District branch in August 1945. It moved from the "Brown Bear" to the "Red Lion" in January 1948. Its Standard was dedicated in July 1949. The branch was dissolved in March 1953.

The Reunions of The Past and Present Association were resumed in July 1946. The programmes were much the same as before the war.

A reunion for those who had served in the 6th Battalion in both world wars was held at Bromley in November 1946. It became an annual event.

The Duchess of Kent consented to be Patron of the association when she became Colonel-in-Chief in May 1947.

The London branch transferred its meetings to the "Spread Eagle" in Pimlico in August 1947. It moved to the "Cranbourn", Leicester Square, in May 1951. By the end of 1953, more than 200 members had been enrolled for this branch.

A Regimental Council was formed on October 1, 1947, by the Colonel of the Regiment (then Brigadier N. I. Whitty) to advise him on the numerous matters on which he had to make a decision. It consisted of the Honorary Colonel of the 4th/5th Battalion, the C.O. and one other rank from each of the Regular and Territorial battalions, the O.C. Depot, the chairman of The Past and Present Association, two representatives of that association, and three serving or retired members nominated by the Colonel of the Regiment.

Throughout the sixteen and a half years that this council was in being, Mr. L. W. Dawson and Mr. P. W. Walker represented The Past and Present Association. The following retired personnel served on the council at various times: Colonel B. L. Clay, Lieutenant-Colonels E. S. Kerr, H. N. Edwards and H. D. Chaplin.

On his retirement in July 1948, Lieutenant-Colonel A. A. Eason became secretary and treasurer of the association.

A dinner for those who had served in the 7th Battalion in both wars was held at the Woodlands Hotel, Gravesend, in April 1949. This became an annual event, usually in London.

A social evening for members of the association took place in the gymnasium at the Depot in October 1949. Thereafter, a similar function was held each year until 1960 inclusive.

The Sevenoaks branch was formed on December 9, 1949. Meetings were at the drill hall in Argyle Road.

The Dartford branch was dissolved towards the end of 1949.

The Catford and District branch opened officially on May 1, 1950. Its first two meetings were at Artillery House in Bromley Road. It then met at the "Ravensbourne" until September 1951, when it moved to the "Prince of Wales" at Forest Hill. In January 1954 its meetings were transferred to the drill hall at Penge, and thence to the Lewisham National Reserve Club in April 1955. Its final move was to the "Railway Signal" at Forest Hill in June 1957. The branch Standard was dedicated on April 26, 1953, at St. George's Church, Forest Hill.

A branch was formed in Guernsey in April 1951 at the "Caves de Bordeaux". There were only about a score of ex-Queen's Own living on the island, and the branch ceased to exist in October 1955.

When the 1st Battalion left Shorncliffe in 1951, the Shorncliffe branch moved from the barracks to the "Fleur-de-Lys" at Sandgate.

The Bromley branch moved from the drill hall in East Street to the United Service Club in the summer of 1952.

After the death of Colonel Palmer in June 1953, Lieutenant-Colonel H. N. Edwards became chairman of the association.

The Coronation Ex-Servicemen's Review in Hyde Park on July 5, 1953, is described in section 1 of chapter 1 above.

The Chatham branch moved from the drill hall in Boundary Road to the "Hare and Hounds" at Rochester in August 1956.

On the amalgamation of The Queen's Own and The Buffs on March 1, 1961, all branches and affiliated battalion associations of The Queen's Own Past and Present Association joined the Regimental Association of The Queen's Own Buffs, The Royal Kent Regiment, as follows:

Branch	Headquarters
Bromley	United Service Club.
Chatham	"The Hare and Hounds", Rochester.
Catford and District	"The Railway Signal", Forest Hill.
Gravesend	Terminus Hotel.
London	"The Cranbourn", Leicester Square.
Maidstone	The Depot Sergeants' Mess.
Sevenoaks	The Drill Hall, Argyle Road.
Shorncliffe	"The Fleur-de-Lys", Sandgate.
Tonbridge and Tunbridge Wells	T.A. Centre, Avebury Avenue, Tonbridge.

Battalion Associations—6th, 7th, 8th, 10th and 11th Battalions, and 20th London.

CHAIRMEN OF THE ASSOCIATION

July 1911-April 1920	Colonel C. E. C. B. Harrison, C.M.G., C.B.E.
April 1920-July 1925	Brig.-General E. A. W. S. Grove, C.B., C.B.E.
July 1925-Nov. 1937	Colonel G. W. Maunsell, C.M.G. .. ..
Nov. 1937-Aug. 1945	Colonel H. D. Buchanan-Dunlop, C.M.G., D.S.O.
Aug. 1945-June 1953	Colonel W. V. Palmer .. ..
Aug. 1953-March 1961	Lieut.-Colonel H. N. Edwards, M.B.E., D.L.

APPENDIX K

Errata in Other Works Concerning The Queen's Own

"A Short Record of the Colours"

Page 21—The 1880-1891 Colours of The 97th were carried until 23rd June 1891, NOT until 25th June 1891.

Page 27—The 1891-1931 Colours of the 2nd Battalion were presented on 23rd June 1891, NOT on 25th June 1891.

Page 28—Colours were presented to the 4th and 5th Battalions (T.F.) on 19th June 1909, NOT in 1908.

"A Short Account of the Origins, Service and Campaigns, 1756-1956"

Page 6—The Sutlej Campaign. 1st para. Delete "and Private Hale", At Ferozeshah Corporal E. Johnson captured two of the enemy Standards.

Page 7—The Sutlej Campaign. 2nd para. At Sobraon a Sikh Colour was captured by Private L. Hale, NOT Sergeant-Major Cantwell.

Page 10—The Indian Mutiny. 2nd para. The garrison of Lucknow was at that time besieged in the Alam Bagh, NOT in the Residency.

Page 14—The 2nd Battalion. 1st para. New Colours were presented on June 23rd 1891, NOT on June 25th 1891.

Page 15—The War in South Africa. 3rd para. The action at Biddulphs Berg was fought on May 29th, NOT on May 28th.

Page 23—Afghanistan. The attack on Fort Spin Baldak took place on May 27th, NOT on May 26th.

Page 24—The 20th Battalion The London Regiment. 2nd para. A King's Colour was presented to the 2/20th on April 10th 1920, NOT on April 20th 1920.

"The Queen's Own Royal West Kent Regiment, 1920-1950"

Page 52—1st para. For the last sentence substitute: "This was the start of The Queen's Own Tent Club".

Page 55—Last para. The invitation to consider themselves permanent Honorary Members of their Mess, which was received by the officers of the 1st Battalion from the officers of the 2nd Battalion The King's Own Scottish Borderers, was an illuminated invitation. It was the invitation sent by the officers of the 1st Battalion that was engraved on a silver plaque.

Page 61—Last para. For the first sentence substitute: "In 1922 the custom began of laying a wreath at the foot of Nelson's Column in London on October 21 each year, in memory of the period in 1794 when The 50th Regiment had served with Nelson in Corsica."

Page 62—3rd para. The 1855 Colours of the 3rd (Militia) Battalion were laid up on July 21, 1929, NOT in July 1928.

Page 68—Last para. The precise date on which the 1891 Colours of the 2nd Battalion were laid up was July 19, 1931.

Page 111—Last para. The precise date on which new Colours were presented to the 1st Battalion was May 17, 1938.

Page 422—1st para. In 1880 the corps in the Greenwich and Blackheath area, together with one at Dartford and one at Bromley, became companies in the 3rd (West Kent) Volunteer Corps, which, in February 1883, was renamed the 2nd Volunteer Battalion The Queen's Own (Royal West Kent Regiment).

Page 422—3rd para. The other companies of the 2nd Volunteer Battalion and the whole of the 3rd Volunteer Battalion were linked together and became the 20th (County of London) Battalion The London Regiment (Blackheath and Woolwich).

Page 429—27th line. The battalion was called out on active service on July 26, 1940, NOT on May 24, 1940.

Page 437—16th line. Kasr-El-Nil Barracks had first been occupied by the 1st Battalion in 1884, NOT in 1882.

Page 478—4th Battalion, Burma. After "Lieutenant J. C. Breaden" put "(General List)". Before he was placed on that list as a Quartermaster, Breaden had been R.Q.M.S. of the 4th Battalion. After the 1939-1945 War he re-enlisted into that Battalion as O.R.Q.M.S. While he was on the General List, he gained an M.B.E. and was twice mentioned in despatches.

Personal Index

Printed in the United Kingdom by
Lightning Source UK Ltd., Milton Keynes
139801UK00001B/33/A

9 781843 426912